Aaron Chalmers is Head of the School of Ministry, Theology and Culture at Tabor Adelaide, South Australia, where he teaches Old Testament, biblical interpretation and Hebrew. His research interests include the history of Israelite religion and the phenomenon of prophecy in ancient Israel. He has had a number of articles published in various scholarly journals, including *Vetus Testamentum*, *Ugarit Forschungen* and *Tyndale Bulletin*. He is the author of *Exploring the Religion of Ancient Israel* (2012), also published by SPCK. He is married to Catherine, and they have four young children.

T0310944

INTERPRETING THE PROPHETS

AARON CHALMERS

First published in Great Britain in 2015

Society for Promoting Christian Knowledge
36 Causton Street
London SW1P 4ST
www.spckpublishing.co.uk

British Library Cataloguing-in-Publication Data
A catalogue record for this book is available from the British Library

ISBN 978–0–281–06904–0
eBook ISBN 978–0–281–06905–7

Typeset by Graphicraft Limited, Hong Kong
First printed in Great Britain by Ashford Colour Press
Subsequently digitally printed in Great Britain

eBook by Graphicraft Limited, Hong Kong

Produced on paper from sustainable forests

Contents

Illustrations

Tables

Preface

The ultimate origins of this book can be traced back to my undergraduate days at Tabor Adelaide when I took a course on interpreting the prophets which was taught by Kevin Jolly. Kevin modelled a concern for social justice and a passion for prophets' scholarship (especially the work of Walter Brueggemann) which was inspiring and pushed me in the direction of further Old Testament studies. It is now my privilege to teach the prophets exegesis subject at Tabor.

My decision to write this text was motivated largely by my frustration at being unable to find a suitable textbook for my students. Most of the standard introductions to the prophetic literature focus largely on issues of content: they tell students when the prophets lived, how their books are structured and what they said. But I wanted my students to be able to do more than just parrot back the interpretations of others – I wanted them to be able to read these wonderful, life-changing books for themselves. Thus, in my teaching I focus on both the knowledge and skills which are required to read the prophets well. This dual focus (knowledge and skills) lies at the heart of this book, and, I believe, distinguishes it from the majority of other introductory works on the prophets which are currently available.

I would like to thank a number of people who have been involved in the process of writing and publishing this book. First of all, I would like to acknowledge Philip Law, Academic Editor at SPCK, for green-lighting this project. Philip has continued to show trust in me and my work, something for which I am truly grateful. In fact, the whole team at SPCK has been a pleasure to work with. I would also like to thank the Revd Dr Stephen Spence, Deputy Principal (Academic) at Tabor Adelaide, who has encouraged a commitment to and space for scholarship and writing at the college where I teach. Also, a number of my Old Testament colleagues, including Prof. John Goldingay (Fuller), Prof. Stephen Cook (Virginia Theological Seminary) and Prof. Brent Sandy (Grace), have generously given of their time to work through drafts of various chapters. Their input has been greatly appreciated. Hopefully, I'll be able to repay the favour one day! I would like to thank the students from my Old Testament prophets exegesis subject at Tabor Adelaide whose questions and reflections have helped to sharpen my own thinking and improve this book. Finally, I would like to thank our long-time family friend, Janelle Palmer, who helped with the indices for both my books.

Writing this book would not have been possible without the love and support of my wife, Catherine, and family, which grew by two in the 18 or so months it took to prepare the manuscript. Having four children four years of age or younger is not necessarily an experience I would recommend to anyone who needs to be critical and creative in his or her work, but we wouldn't have it any other way.

This book is dedicated to my parents, Brian and Joanne Chalmers, who instilled in me from a young age a love of God and a love of learning.

Abbreviations

ABRL	Anchor Bible Reference Library
ALASP	Abhandlungen zur Literatur Alt-Syrien-Palästinas und Mesopotamiens
ANET	Pritchard, J. (ed.), *Ancient Near Eastern Texts Relating to the Old Testament*, 3rd edn with supp. Princeton: Princeton University Press, 1969.
BRS	Biblical Resource Series
BS	Biblical Seminar
CHANE	Culture and History of the Ancient Near East
COS	Hallo, W. (gen. ed.), *The Context of Scripture*, vols 1–3. Leiden: Brill, 2003.
GBSOTS	Guides to Biblical Scholarship Old Testament Series
IBT	Interpreting Biblical Texts
JSOT	Journal for the Study of the Old Testament
KTU	Dietrich, M., O. Loretz and J. Sanmartín, *The Cuneiform Alphabetic Texts from Ugarit, Ras Ibn Hani and Other Places*, 2nd edn, ALASP 8. Münster: Ugarit Verlag, 1995.
LAI	Library of Ancient Israel
LXX	Septuagint
MT	Masoretic Text
NSBT	New Studies in Biblical Theology
OTL	Old Testament Library
SBL	Society of Biblical Literature
SBLABS	Society of Biblical Literature Archaeology and Biblical Studies
SBLRBS	Society of Biblical Literature Resources for Biblical Study
SBLWAW	Society of Biblical Literature Writings from the Ancient World
SBTS	Sources for Biblical and Theological Study
SHANE	Studies in the History of the Ancient Near East
SWBAS	Social World of Biblical Antiquity Series
UBT	Understanding Biblical Themes
WBC	Word Biblical Commentary
WJKP	Westminster John Knox Press

Introduction

They [the prophets] have a queer way of talking, like people who, instead of proceeding in an orderly manner, ramble off from one thing to the next, so that you cannot make head or tail of them or see what they are getting at.
(Martin Luther, cited in von Rad, 1965: 33)

The prophetic books of the Old Testament contain some of the most awe-inspiring, confronting and compelling passages in the entire Bible.[1] From their uncompromising proclamation of God's work in salvation and judgement to their incessant and pressing calls for social justice, they speak with a power and urgency which continues to challenge the Church and its witness in the world today.

Yet many Christians remain confused and frustrated by these works. They are full of dramatic imagery whose meaning is not always clear. Sometimes there appears to be little rhyme or reason in the flow of their thought. They include numerous references to events from Israel's history and life, the significance of which we do not grasp. It is perhaps little wonder, therefore, that the prophets are so frequently misunderstood and misapplied by many within the Church, conservative and liberal alike.

After teaching courses on the Old Testament prophets for a number of years, I have come to the conclusion that what readers need is a basic conceptual 'framework' for understanding these books. This framework is not provided by standard introductions to the prophets, which characteristically focus on issues such as the date, structure and key themes of the various books. While such information is important (after all, the prophetic books are occasional literature, and thus need to be understood within their specific historical context), such an approach does not end up equipping people with the necessary skills they need for interpreting the prophetic books themselves. It gives people the fish but does not teach them how to be fishermen.

---

[1] It should be recognized that the label 'prophets' is used with different nuances in Jewish and Christian traditions. In Christian tradition, the title is used to refer to the four major prophets (Isaiah, Jeremiah, Ezekiel and Daniel) and 12 minor prophets (Hosea – Malachi) (the adjectives 'major' and 'minor' refer to the relative length of the books, not their importance). In Jewish tradition, the title is used to refer to a larger portion of the canon: the former prophets (Joshua, Judges, Samuel and Kings) and latter prophets (Isaiah, Jeremiah, Ezekiel and the Book of the Twelve). To put it simply, the section of Scripture referred to by Christians as 'the prophets' is broadly equivalent to the Jewish latter prophets. In this book I employ the labels 'the prophets' and 'the prophetic literature' according to traditional Christian usage. Another title I sometimes employ to refer to this group is 'writing prophets'. It needs to be recognized, however, that this label is potentially misleading – we do not actually know who was responsible for composing the prophetic words in written form. For further discussion of this issue, see Chapter 1. These prophets are also sometimes referred to as the 'classical prophets' (in contrast to the pre-classical prophets who were operative in the period from Moses through to the beginning of Amos' ministry).

1

In this book, therefore, I take a different approach. My goal is to equip readers with the knowledge and skills they need to be competent and faithful interpreters of the prophetic books themselves. In order to do this, I begin by looking at the nature of both Israel's prophets and the books that were associated with them. In standard introductions, the latter is often neglected at the expense of a detailed discussion of the former. This imbalance is problematic, especially when we realize that our goal is not to exegete the prophetic personages but the prophetic *books*. Building a solid foundational understanding of the nature of both these elements – prophet and book – is therefore essential if we wish to interpret these works well; all kinds of problems can arise as a result of faulty or inadequate conceptions regarding the character of either of these. In fact, such misconceptions can potentially be more harmful than lack of knowledge because they distort our reading of the biblical text (we go looking for things that the author never intended us to look for) and blind us to our ignorance (we think we know more than we actually do).

The majority of this book is devoted to the three key 'worlds' (or contexts) which we need to consider to interpret these books well. They include:

1 *the historical world*: the time, place and situation the prophets were addressing;
2 *the theological world*: the beliefs, ideologies and assumptions, especially regarding God, the Israelite king and the Israelite people, which shaped the prophets' writings;
3 *the rhetorical world*: how the prophets effectively used language and shaped their material in order to persuade and influence their audience.

In each chapter I provide an overview of these worlds, before presenting some guidelines for how we should read the prophetic texts in the light of these. I also include a discussion of some of the common interpretive mistakes associated with each one. By the end of each chapter, readers should have a better idea of what they need to do (and avoid) when interpreting these texts which come from a very different time and place from our own.

Chapter 5 is devoted to interpreting the apocalyptic texts from the Old Testament. Although related to prophecy, apocalyptic is generally recognized as a distinct genre with its own emphases and set of literary 'rules'. An awareness of these can help the reader avoid some of the common interpretive mistakes associated with this challenging genre.

In the final chapter we will consider how to preach from the prophets in an authentic, faithful and responsible fashion. This element is neglected in most standard introductory works on the prophets, which generally seem content to leave the prophets as God's messengers for ancient Israel, perhaps assuming that on this basis the reader will somehow be able to make the jump from the world of the Old Testament to the contemporary world. Such an omission, however, is unhelpful, especially given the unique homiletical challenges these texts raise and the fact that the majority of people who want to learn more about interpreting the prophets are doing so with the goal that they might hear and speak God's word to God's people today.

Interpreting the prophets well is not an easy task. Yet it is an essential one. The prophets take up about as much space in the Bible as the New Testament does. To ignore them, therefore, is to cut ourselves off from a significant portion of God's revelation to his people. It is my hope that this book will help to open up these texts so that through them the people of God might encounter and be confronted once again by the powerful and dynamic words of the living and speaking God.

1

What is a prophet and what is a prophetic book?

1.1 Introduction

Given that we are focusing on interpreting the *prophetic* literature in this book, it seems appropriate to begin our journey with a discussion of what an Israelite prophet actually was. This is not as straightforward as it may at first seem. Since 'prophet' is a label which we still employ today to refer to various individuals, it is all too easy for us to allow contemporary conceptions to colour our understanding of ancient usage. This is problematic on a number of levels, as I will explain below. Furthermore, our attempts to come up with a concise definition are complicated by the presence of significant variations within the phenomenon of prophecy itself in ancient Israel. This makes it difficult to come up with useful, unifying, overarching statements. As Goldingay has recognized:

> Defining prophecy is a notoriously difficult matter. Any description of prophecy that has bite will turn out not to apply to every First Testament prophet, let alone to prophets in the New Testament. A definition that does apply to every prophet will turn out to be somewhat vacuous and/or apply to people other than prophets. (2011: 311)

In spite of the difficulty, however, I believe that such an attempt is worth the effort – developing an accurate picture of what a prophet was in ancient Israel provides a context for better understanding the writings with which they were associated.

In the second part of this chapter we will consider the journey from prophetic personage to prophetic book, a journey which may be longer and more complex than we assume. As exegetes of the biblical text, our primary focus is not the prophets per se but the books that bear their name. Therefore, it is worth considering the process by which the primarily spoken words of the prophets became the written words which we now have before us.

1.2 What is a prophet? Modern answers

The following three quotes provide examples of three distinct ways the word 'prophet' is commonly used today:

> If I have eschewed the word prophet, I do not wish to attribute to myself such lofty title at the present time, for whoever is called a prophet now was once

called a seer; since a prophet, my son, is properly speaking one who sees distant things through a natural knowledge of all creatures. And it can happen that the prophet bringing about the perfect light of prophecy may make manifest things both human and divine, because this cannot be done otherwise, given that the effects of predicting the future extend far off into time.

(Nostradamus, *The Prophecies*)[1]

We knew no one man had killed the prophet. Rather, the combined weight of racism and an absence of moral courage had crushed him. A constitution ignored, laws denied, these were the weapons. America pulled the trigger.

(Golden, 1983: 14 about Martin Luther King)

I have proved by how many prophecies the coming of the Word of God to men was foretold, and that it was announced by the Hebrew prophets whence He should come, and where and how He should be seen by men on earth, and that He was actually the Person, the eternal pre-existent Son of God, Whom we have learned to recognize by the other names of God and Lord and Chief Captain, and Angel of Great Counsel and High Priest.

(Eusebius, 'Introduction', *Demonstratio Evangelica*
(*The Proof of the Gospel*), Book 8)[2]

The first quote suggests that a prophet is primarily a *predictor of the future*. According to Nostradamus (who is himself reluctant to accept the title), the defining feature of a prophet is that he or she is able to foretell events in the (distant) future. Such a person possesses unique insight into the unfolding of history. A cursory glance at the shelf labelled 'prophecy' in your local Christian bookstore will show that such an understanding is widespread – the biblical prophets are commonly viewed as providing detailed descriptions of events associated with the end times.

The second quote suggests that a prophet is primarily a *social reformer*. It is common for the label 'prophet' to be applied to political and social activists whose primary goal is to bring about change within their society. Thus, Golden refers to Martin Luther King Jr simply as 'the prophet' (see Fig. 1.1 overleaf). In this case, the biblical prophets are viewed as early advocates of social justice and defenders of the marginalized.

The third quote suggests that an Old Testament prophet is primarily a *herald of Jesus*. Eusebius' statement implies that the role of Israel's prophets was to announce and foretell the coming of the Messiah (see Fig. 1.2 overleaf). Although perhaps not so common today, this understanding has a long history in Christian circles, stretching back to the authors of the New Testament itself, and being particularly popular with the early Church Fathers.

Although each of these understandings carries an element of truth, it would be problematic to assume that they provide an adequate framework for understanding the prophets of ancient Israel. Occasionally the prophets do foretell future events, but this is not as common as we might expect. Fee and

[1] <http://en.wikiquote.org/wiki/Nostradamus>, accessed 23 September 2013.
[2] <http://www.earlychristianwritings.com/fathers/eusebius_de_10_book8.html>, accessed 23 September 2013.

Figure 1.1 Martin Luther King Jr is often referred to as a prophet
National Archives and Records Administration / Wikimedia Commons.

Stuart have suggested that 'Less than 2 percent of Old Testament prophecy is messianic. Less than 5 percent specifically describes the new-covenant age. Less than 1 percent concerns events yet to come in our time' (2003: 182). According to these figures less than 8 per cent of Old Testament prophecy is concerned with the time of Jesus through to the present – the *vast* majority of Old Testament prophecy (more than 92 per cent!) addressed Israel's immediate

Figure 1.2 'Isaiah' from von Carolsfeld's *Die Bibel in Bildern*. This image clearly portrays the prophet as a predictor of Christ's birth, death and victory over Satan

Woodcut from J. S. von Carolsfeld, *Die Bibel in Bildern*, Leipzig: Wigand, 1860. Wikimedia Commons.

or imminent situation. To suggest that the prophets are primarily foretellers, particularly of events in our day, is therefore to emphasize only a small element of their role.

Furthermore, although the prophets are clearly concerned with social reform and justice (see, for example, Amos 5.12; Isa. 1.16–17), there is a theological basis and dimension to their work which is not necessarily implied in the second contemporary understanding.[3] The prophets' desire to see change in the economic and political workings of the nation is a part of their larger vision for the transformation of the people of God as a whole (including their religious life), with all this based on a certain vision of God and his requirements of his people. Contemporary social reform movements do not

---

[3] Of course, this is not to deny that there may be a theological basis for some contemporary social reforming movements. The work of Martin Luther King Jr, for instance, was driven by his Christian beliefs. Instead, I am suggesting that our contemporary use of the title does not necessarily imply this dimension or basis.

necessarily have this theological 'edge'. A second, related limitation of this understanding concerns their intended audience: Israel's prophets are primarily called to address the people of God (Israel and/or Judah), whereas social reform movements usually have a wider target, being concerned with society as a whole.[4]

Finally, although the New Testament authors recognize that the prophets do occasionally speak in ways which anticipate Jesus (see, for example, Matt. 2.5–6 quoting Mic. 5.2, and John 12.14–15 quoting Zech. 9.9), the figures from Fee and Stuart cited above indicate that this is hardly central to or the defining element of their ministry. A reliance on contemporary usage of the term 'prophet', therefore, is likely to result in an anachronistic understanding of the nature and roles of Israel's prophets. Thus, we will need to turn to the text of the Old Testament itself, drawing on comparative ancient Near Eastern parallels where relevant, if we wish to develop a more accurate picture.

Figure 1.3 A terracotta relief of Ištar holding her symbol (early second millennium BC). The goddess Ištar of Arbela is frequently referred to in the Neo-Assyrian prophecies

© Marie-Lan Nguyen / Wikimedia Commons.

---

[4] For further discussion, see Chapter 6.

Have you considered?
PROPHECY AS AN ANCIENT NEAR EASTERN PHENOMENON

It is clear that the phenomenon of prophecy was not unique to Israel but was, in fact, widespread throughout the ancient Near East. This is a reality which the Old Testament itself recognizes. For example, the prophet Jeremiah urges rulers from the neighbouring lands of Edom, Moab, Ammon and the Phoenician cities who may have been considering rebellion against Nebuchadnezzar, king of Babylon, not to heed their prophets, diviners and other intermediaries (Jer. 27.1–15).

Prophetic texts have been uncovered at a number of ancient Near Eastern sites, including Mari (from the eighteenth century BC) and Nineveh (from the seventh century BC). The documents from Mari include approximately 50 letters sent to the king (usually Zimri-lim) by various officials and administrators, containing messages from various intermediaries claiming divine inspiration. Such figures may refer to themselves as being 'sent' by the deity, and their messages often begin with the formula 'Thus says [the god *x*]' or a similar equivalent, with the deity characteristically speaking in the first person. For example, a certain Malik-Dagan is commissioned by the god Dagan: 'Now go, I send you. Thus you shall speak to Zimrilim saying: "Send me your messengers and lay your full report before me . . ."' (cited in Blenkinsopp, 1996: 44). These documents almost exclusively focus on the king's affairs (they were found as part of a larger royal archive), including his military activities, cultic issues and the need to maintain justice.*

The documents from Nineveh witness to significant prophetic activity within the Neo-Assyrian Empire (see Fig. 1.3). As with the documents from Mari, the Neo-Assyrian texts were part of a royal archive and thus focus primarily on the king's activity. It appears that in the majority of cases the prophetic message was prompted by a crisis situation (often involving a military, political or succession concern) which resulted in the king complaining to or enquiring of a deity. The divine response is almost always a message of reassurance, emphasizing the deity's power and reliability, giving directions on political and military matters, and assuring the king of success in his undertakings. The phrase 'Fear not!' is common. For example:

> [Esarh]addon, king of the lands, fear [not]! . . . I am the great Lady, I am Ištar of Arbela who throw your enemies before your feet. Have I spoken to you any words that you could not rely upon? I am Ištar of Arbela, I will flay your enemies and deliver them up to you. I am Ištar of Arbela, I go before you and behind you.   (Nissinen, 2003: 102)

These documents also point to the existence of a significant number of female prophets.

Outside the texts from Mari and Nineveh we encounter references to prophecy in:

1 an Old Aramaic inscription of Zakkur, king of Hamath and Luash (c.800 BC), located in northern Syria;

---

* Huffmon has argued that recently discovered texts from Mari point to a wider, public audience for the prophets. These texts indicate that the prophets would occasionally summon the elders and speak to a public assembly, not just the king (1997: 18).

2　a plaster inscription from Tell Deir 'Alla, which was probably part of the Ammonite kingdom and is dated c.700 BC – this contains a reference to Balaam, son of Beor, a 'visionary of the gods' (*ḥāzēh 'ilāhīn*), who is probably the same figure mentioned in the Old Testament (Num. 22—24);

3　the Egyptian 'Story of Wen-Amun' (c. tenth century BC), which narrates an episode involving ecstatic prophecy from Byblos in Phoenicia.

For further discussion of ancient Near Eastern prophecy and prophetic texts, see Nissinen, 2003; Stökl, 2012b.

1.3 What is a prophet? Old Testament answers[5]

Have you considered?
THE SIZE OF THE PHENOMENON OF PROPHECY IN ANCIENT ISRAEL

When I ask my students to name some Old Testament prophets, common responses include Isaiah, Jeremiah, Ezekiel and perhaps Amos. In other words, we tend to focus on those prophets who have books attributed to them. But we need to be aware that these individuals account for only a very small (and often anomalous) minority of the total number of prophets who were at work in ancient Israel (Blenkinsopp, 1996: 47). In addition to the 55 or so named prophets in the Old Testament, the text itself recognizes the presence of literally *hundreds* of other prophets who remain unnamed (e.g. 1 Kings 22.6). Furthermore, even the earliest of our canonical prophets (Amos and Hosea) see themselves as standing within the context of a much wider and older phenomenon (cf. Amos 2.11–12; Hos. 6.5). In short, the canonical prophets provide only a very small window into the nature of prophecy as it was found within ancient Israel.

Before we can come to grips with what it meant to be a prophet in ancient Israel, we need to realize that the phenomenon of prophecy itself was, in fact, very broad and quite diverse. The prophets conceived of their ministry in different ways, operated in different fashions and came from different backgrounds. The diversity which was present within the prophetic movement means that it is difficult to come up with generalizations pertaining to the prophets, and that any sweeping statements which we do formulate are likely to be open to debate. Nevertheless, some degree of generalization is both possible and warranted; after all, the people of ancient Israel themselves seem to have viewed these figures as belonging to a common *genus*. Given that this is a book on interpreting the prophetic writings, and not the phenomenon of prophecy in ancient

---

[5] Much of the material in this section is drawn from Chalmers, 2012: 39–66.

Israel in general, I have chosen to focus on those characteristics which are particularly pertinent for understanding the so-called writing prophets.[6]

Going deeper:
THE HEBREW TITLES OF ISRAEL'S PROPHETS

The Old Testament authors use four main labels or titles to refer to the individuals we dub prophets: *nābî'* (prophet), *rō'eh* (seer), *ḥōzeh* (seer), and *'îš 'ĕlōhîm* (man of God). At one stage these titles may have had their own distinctive connotations. For example, Blenkinsopp has suggested that the title 'man of God', which we find applied to key early prophetic figures such as Samuel, Elijah and Elisha, originally denoted 'a person of preternatural and potentially dangerous power; recall, for example, how Samson's mother, cowed by the awe-inspiring appearance of her heavenly visitor, took him to be a man of God (Judg. 13: 6, 8)' (1995: 125–6).[*] *nābî'* appears to have been related to the Akkadian word *nabû(m)* ('to name, proclaim, call') and thus may have meant 'speaker, proclaimer' (understood in an active sense) or 'one who is named, called' (understood in a passive sense).[†]

It would be unwise, however, to conclude too much purely based on the meaning and usage of these various labels. Overall, it is relatively difficult for the modern interpreter to detect any unique nuances preserved in the Old Testament's usage of such descriptors.[‡] For example, within David's court, Gad is described as a *ḥōzeh* while his colleague Nathan is a *nābî'*, yet there is no discernible difference in the roles the two played. In Amos 7.10–17 the priest Amaziah calls Amos a *ḥōzeh* to which Amos replies that he is *not* a *nābî'*, 'as though the two terms were, for all practical purposes, indistinguishable' (Hutton, 1994: 116).[§] Thus scholars speak of a process of flattening out, whereby the individual designations lost their distinctive nuances and *nābî'* increasingly became used as a catch-all term to refer to the various forms of Israelite prophetic intermediation. This process is suggested by 1 Samuel 9.9 which implies that even from a relatively early date any clear role-distinction associated with the various titles had been forgotten: 'the one who is now called a prophet (*nābî'*) was formerly called a seer (*rō'eh*)'.[**]

---

[*] Blenkinsopp goes on to suggest that, in contrast to seer, there is no indication of a cultic connection for a man of God and that people who held such a title were probably itinerant (1995: 125–6).

[†] Most scholars prefer the passive option. For more details see Müller, 1998: 129–50.

[‡] A recent attempt is that of Petersen, 1997: 24–30.

[§] Other texts which suggest a close relationship between *ḥōzeh* and *nābî'* include 2 Kings 17.13; Isa. 29.10; Mic. 3.7.

[**] Furthermore, in 1 Sam. 9—10 the same figure, Samuel, is referred to as both a *rō'eh* and *'îš 'ĕlōhîm*, suggesting the titles' synonymy.

---

[6] For example, I have omitted any discussion of the prophets as miracle workers as Isaiah is the only classical prophet associated with such activity. For further details see Chalmers, 2012: 62. It should be acknowledged that while I have employed the title 'writing prophets' in this chapter to refer to those prophets who are associated with particular books, the label itself is potentially misleading. For a discussion of the written composition of the prophetic books, see 1.4.1.

1.3.1 A prophet was a member of the divine council

A number of Israel's prophets claimed to have stood in the presence of God and those supernatural creatures who composed God's deliberating council. This is a unique claim on the part of the prophets – no other individual is ever described as being allowed to attend God's council meeting (Meier, 2009: 21).

So what did this 'divine council' look like? The text which provides the most detailed description is 1 Kings 22.19–23. Here the Lord is portrayed as sitting on his throne with all the 'host of heaven' in attendance surrounding him. These beings interact with the Lord (vv. 20–21) and carry out his will on the earth (v. 22). A similar picture is presented in Job 1—2 where the council members are referred to literally as 'sons of God' (or 'heavenly beings' NRSV; cf. Pss. 29.1; 82.6; 89.7, etc.). The heavenly realm appears to be depicted as operating along lines similar to an ancient Near Eastern royal court with the monarch surrounded by counsellors and envoys that advise the king and perform his will.

Various texts from the Old Testament suggest that prophets could play a threefold role within the divine council:

1 Prophets could function as *observers* of the council – this seems to be the case for Micaiah in 1 Kings 22. Here the prophet simply observes the proceedings of the council and reports its deliberations to the king of Israel but does not get involved in any way.
2 Prophets could function as *'advisers'* to God – some prophets take a more active role in the workings of the divine council, engaging with God regarding the decisions he will make. The best example of this appears to be Amos. In Amos 7.1–9 the prophet dialogues with God concerning his proposed judgement on the northern kingdom and actually prompts God to consider alternative courses of action.[7]
3 Prophets could function as *envoys* for the council – the best example of this is Isaiah 6. Here the prophet is given a vision of the divine council with God enthroned and seraphs in attendance (see Fig. 1.4). Of particular importance is verse 8. In this verse the Lord appears to be addressing the divine council (note the parallels with 1 Kings 22.20–21), seeking someone who will carry out his will. Isaiah responds and accepts the role – he is now an envoy for the Lord.

The importance of access to the divine council by Israel's prophets is emphasized by Jeremiah. In fact, he makes this a key criterion by which one is able to distinguish genuine prophets from their counterfeits (Jer. 23.16–22).

---

[7] At the same time, however, it must be kept in mind that whenever we encounter extended descriptions of the divine council, God is typically described as being seated on his throne (cf. Isa. 6.1; Ezek. 1.26). This is 'an emphatic reminder that the cosmos is not a democracy and that God is in control' (Meier, 2009: 22).

Figure 1.4 Relief depicting a six-winged goddess (or a woman wearing a long, fringed robe with six wings) from the temple-palace at Tel Halaf, reminiscent of the description of the seraphs in Isaiah 6.2

© Walters Art Museum / Wikimedia Commons.

A true prophet stands in the divine council – he or she has access to the transcendent workings of the Deity – and thus speaks God's word. False prophets, however, are unable to gain admission to this council and thus can only speak their own word.

1.3.2 A prophet was called by God

A number of Israel's writing prophets highlight a unique encounter with the Lord, often referred to in the secondary literature as the prophet's 'call', as the determinative factor in generating their prophetic ministry. Key accounts of such call experiences include Isaiah 6, Jeremiah 1, Ezekiel 1—3, and Moses in Exodus 3 (cf. Amos 7.15). This experience of divine calling appears to come unexpectedly and marks a decisive transition point within the prophet's life. After receiving the call, the prophet understands that he or she is specially set apart by God in order to fulfil a specific task or role.

What did this call experience actually involve? The stylized literary reports which have been preserved suggest that a typical prophetic call experience might have taken place along the following lines:

1 *God appears to and confronts the individual.* This divine appearance could take a number of different forms. For example, God appears to Moses in the midst of the burning bush, Isaiah sees the Lord sitting on his throne with seraphs in attendance, while Ezekiel is confronted by the radiant glory of the Lord astride the divine chariot.

2 *God commissions the prophet.* The prophet is characteristically told two things: to whom he or she must speak (i.e. the intended audience) and what to speak or do (i.e. the basic content of their message). For example, Moses must bring the Israelites out of Egypt, while Jeremiah's message is summarized in six antithetic verbs: 'to pluck up and to pull down, to destroy and to over-throw, to build and to plant' (Jer. 1.10b; cf. 18.7–9; 24.6, etc) (see Fig. 1.5).

3 *The prophet responds.* While Isaiah volunteers to fulfil the divine commission, this reaction is anomalous. More often than not, the prophet's initial response is negative in tone. In fact, prophets may object to their calling, usually on the basis of their perceived unworthiness or inadequacy to fulfil the divine commission they have been given. For example, Moses' initial response to the sweeping divine declaration that he will be sent to Pharaoh to bring the Israelites out of Egypt is not to embrace the divine mandate but to cry 'Who am I?' (Exod. 3.11). Likewise, when told that he has been

Figure 1.5 'The call of Jeremiah' from von Carolsfeld's *Die Bibel in Bildern*
Woodcut from J. S. von Carolsfeld, *Die Bibel in Bildern*, Leipzig: Wigand, 1860. Wikimedia Commons.

appointed as a prophet to the nations, Jeremiah laments that he does not know how to speak for he is 'only a boy' (Jer. 1.6). Such objections, however, are usually quickly countered.

4 *The prophet is prepared or equipped for his or her ministry.* Again this activity can take a variety of different forms. Isaiah's mouth is cleansed to make it fit to utter the divine word, the Lord touches Jeremiah's mouth, putting the divine word inside him, and Ezekiel eats a scroll with writing on both sides of it. All three accounts, however, emphasize the external and objective character of the prophetic word – 'what a prophet speaks does not come from himself but from God' (Lindblom, 1963: 189). This preparation may also include an element of divine reassurance, with the Lord promising to be with the prophet no matter what situation he or she may face.

Going deeper:
THE MINOR PROPHETS AND DIVINE CALLING

Jeremiah implies that divine calling was an essential qualification of the true prophets of Israel. According to Jeremiah 14.14 the false prophets are marked out by the fact that 'I [Yahweh] did not send them, nor did I command them or speak to them' (cf. Deut. 18.20; Ezek.13.6). Thus, while no exact equivalents to the prophetic call accounts are found in the minor prophets (perhaps a result of the much shorter length of these works), it is quite possible that these prophets also experienced a similar divine encounter and commissioning which generated their ministry.

1.3.3 A prophet communicated the word of the Lord

The primary function of Israel's prophets was to reveal the Deity's word and will to humanity. The actual content of this revelation could be quite diverse. It may have included responses to queries regarding an individual's illness, proclamations centring on cultic faithfulness, and teaching the king and people, the leaders and populace, to serve the Deity in an appropriate fashion (Miller, 2000: 186).

Have you considered?
WERE ANY OF THE WRITING PROPHETS COURT PROPHETS?

Ancient Near Eastern and biblical evidence points to the existence of so-called 'court prophets' who were formally connected to the royal court and whose primary role was to act as consultants for the king, bringing the divine input they required before significant decisions were made.* For example, when facing the armies of

---
* See also the example of David who 'consults' with Nathan about his desire to construct a temple for the Lord (2 Sam. 7.1–3).

the Aramaean king Barhaddad, Zakkur, king of Hamuth and Luash, prayed to
the god Baalshamyn who answered him through 'seers' (*ḥzyn*) and 'messengers'.
Well-known examples of court prophets in the Old Testament include Nathan and
Gad, with the latter explicitly referred to as 'David's seer' (2 Sam. 24.11). Although
some of Israel's writing prophets, especially Isaiah and Jeremiah, came into
contact with the nation's kings as part of their ministry, there is little evidence to
suggest that any held a formal position within the Israelite bureaucracy.

We may think that the prophets took the initiative in approaching their
audience to deliver the divinely inspired word. But there is a lot of evidence
to suggest that the reverse could also be true – sometimes the word of the
Lord would be sought out by an individual or group of people who took
the initiative in directly approaching the prophet. This individual or group
may have had a question which required a response from God or may have
been seeking divine guidance on a specific issue. For example, some of the
elders of Israel approached the prophet Ezekiel in order to enquire of the
Lord (Ezek. 20.1; cf. Zech. 7). This custom of directly approaching a prophet
or group of prophets to discover the divine will seems to have been a common
practice of Israel's kings. In terms of the writing prophets, Isaiah was consulted
by Hezekiah during the Assyrian invasion of Judah (Isa. 37.1–7). Similarly,
Zedekiah sought out Jeremiah on a number of occasions as the Babylonian
army besieged Jerusalem (Jer. 21; 37.3–10). In addition, prophets were often
consulted by the reigning monarch before a military campaign in order to
determine its chance of success (e.g. 1 Kings 22).[8]

While individuals, including Israel's kings, could come to a prophet to seek
out God's will, more often than not, the writing prophets were directed by
God to take the initiative and directly approach their audience. For example,
Amos travelled from his hometown of Tekoa in Judah to Bethel in order to
address the problems that plagued the northern kingdom (Amos 7.13). Likewise,
Jeremiah was directed to go to the gate of the Lord's house to deliver his
famous Temple sermon (Jer. 7.1–2). In this regard, Israel's prophets have been
likened to ancient diplomats or messengers who were responsible for trans-
porting an important message or command from one individual (or in the
case of the prophets, the Deity) to another.

A key text which sheds light on the role of the prophet as a messenger is
2 Kings 18 (Lang, 1983: 70–1). This describes how, in 701 BC, the Assyrian
military juggernaut overran the tiny state of Judah, capturing all the significant towns before eventually laying siege to Jerusalem. As the Assyrian army
sat encamped around Jerusalem, a period of feverish diplomacy between

---

[8] This practice of kings consulting their prophets before engaging in a military battle was not restricted
to Israel. For example, the annals of the Assyrian kings Sargon and Sennacherib mention the receipt of
oracles from the god Ashur which led to the king fighting and defeating his opponent.

Figure 1.6 The Assyrians besiege a town with archers and a wheeled battering ram (c.865–860 BC)

Hall, H. *Babylonian and Assyrian Sculpture in the British Museum*. Paris: Les Éditions G. van Oest, 1928.

Hezekiah, the king of Judah, and Sennacherib, the king of Assyria, ensued (see Fig. 1.6). Instead of personally meeting and engaging in direct negotiations, however, these kings sent a series of messengers, envoys and diplomats who communicated their will to the enemy. The kings never negotiated in person but made use of their delegates.

The similarity between the recorded speeches of the ancient envoys and the prophet Isaiah is particularly noticeable. The use of a common messenger formula highlights the close relationship between the role of envoy and that of prophet.[9] For example, in 2 Kings 18.31 the messengers of the Assyrian king declare, 'Thus says the king of Assyria . . .', and in 2 Kings 19.3 the messenger of Hezekiah begins his speech to Isaiah with 'Thus says Hezekiah . . .'. The correspondence with Isaiah's response in 2 Kings 19.6 is immediate and obvious: 'Thus says [Yahweh] . . .'. This clear similarity suggests that the prophet viewed himself along the lines of an envoy sent by the divine King, Yahweh, whose primary task was to bring the message of the divine King to human beings:

> That is why he does not talk about his god but in the words of his god: the prophet bears, corresponding to the style of the diplomats, not his own message but that of his lord; this is kept in the first person which is typical of prophetic literature. (Lang, 1983: 71)

As with ancient envoys, the spoken word was clearly the most popular medium for communicating the divine message. This is shown by the fact that the prophetic books are filled with oracles which the prophets *proclaimed*. Nevertheless, spoken discourse was not the only medium of communication

---

[9] The close relationship between messengers and prophets is further reinforced by the use of a similar commissioning formula ('Go to . . . and say . . .'). This is found, for example, as part of Jeremiah's commission: 'go to all to whom I send you, and you shall speak whatever I command you' (Jer. 1.7; cf. Gen. 32.3–4).

that a prophet had at his or her disposal. A number of prophets, both writing and non-writing, engage in symbolic actions whereby the prophet 'acts out' in various, sometimes startling, ways the word he or she has received from the Lord. Matthews and Benjamin (1993: 215–16) suggest that the symbolic actions of Israel's prophets belong to three main categories:

1 *Single dramatic gestures*: for example, when Jeremiah buries his loincloth in the bank of the Euphrates River as a sign of the imminent judgement of Judah (Jer. 13.1–11). Most of the prophetic symbolic actions belong to this category.
2 *Austere practices or ascetism*: for example, when Jeremiah refuses to marry or attend funerals or celebrations as a way of proclaiming the widespread death which is about to come on God's people (Jer. 16.1–13).
3 *Silent actions or crafts of another, identified by the prophet, like a docent*: for example, when Jeremiah draws the attention of his audience to vintners jugging their wine and connects this with the coming drunkenness and destruction of the inhabitants of Jerusalem (Jer. 13.12–14).

In each case, the action is initiated by Yahweh in exactly the same way as the spoken word was given to the prophet. Thus Lindblom (1963: 172) refers to such activities as '*verbum visibile*', a visible word.

1.3.4 A prophet was an intercessor

Intercessory prayer appears to have been a key role of some of Israel's prophets, but not all. Strong evidence for an association between intercession and the prophetic office is suggested by the reference to Abraham in Genesis 20.7 as a prophet 'who will pray for you [i.e. Abimelech] and you shall live'. In this text Abraham is explicitly identified as a prophet on the basis of his ability to intercede before God, suggesting that, at least in some circles, such activity was believed to be a characteristic part of a prophet's responsibilities (Wilson, 1980: 151).

Key prophets such as Moses (Exod. 32), Samuel (1 Sam. 12.19, 23), Amos and Jeremiah intercede on a number of occasions to avert divine wrath from coming upon the nation (see Fig. 1.7). Amos appeals to the Lord on two occasions, and this results in the Lord relenting and not bringing about the judgement he had threatened (Amos 7.1–6). In a similar vein, Jeremiah is requested by the king and people not simply to enquire of the Lord, but to intercede for them and their well-being (Jer. 37.3; 42.2, 4; cf. 7.16; 27.18).[10]

While these are the only named prophets who are recorded as engaging in acts of intercession, the book of Ezekiel suggests that holders of the prophetic office were expected to pray for the people. This becomes clear when we compare Ezekiel 22.30 with 13.4–5. In the former passage, Yahweh

---

[10] 'Only by understanding the signal importance of the prophet's role as the community's chief intercessor can we appreciate … Jeremiah's pain at being disallowed by God to perform his intercessory role for a time (Jer 7:16; 14:11; 15:1–2)' (Hutton, 1994: 123).

Figure 1.7 Limestone stele depicting Nakhtimen praying to the Egyptian goddess Meretseger portrayed as a snake
© Marie-Lan Nguyen / Wikimedia Commons.

claims to have 'sought for anyone among them who would repair the wall and stand in the breach before me on behalf of the land, so that I would not destroy it; but I found no one'. In the latter passage, the Lord explicitly identifies the ones who were meant to be responsible for 'repairing the walls' and 'standing in the breach' as Israel's prophets. Thus, while intercessory activity was not limited to the prophets (priests could also serve in this capacity, offering up prayers and sacrifices to God on the people's behalf), it is evident that this was a role which both God and their compatriots expected them to play.

1.3.5 A prophet was a sentinel

One of the key images used by Ezekiel to describe his ministry is that of a watchman or sentinel: 'So you, mortal, I have made a sentinel for the house of Israel; whenever you hear a word from my mouth, you shall give them warning from me' (Ezek. 33.7; cf. 3.17). Sentinels are mentioned in a number of Old Testament narrative passages, including 1 Samuel 14.16; 2 Samuel 13.34; 18.24–27; and 2 Kings 9.17–20. They were typically stationed on an elevated location (e.g. on a wall, tower, or the roof of a city gate) which provided them with a vantage point to observe the surrounding terrain

Figure 1.8 A reconstructed Israelite watchtower
Courtesy Dr Ed Bez, Biblical Botanical Gardens Society.

(see Fig. 1.8). Their role is outlined in Ezekiel 33.1–6: they were responsible for seeing attacking armies before the other people, sounding the alarm (i.e. blowing the *šôpār*) and warning the people of the impending attack. In a similar fashion, Ezekiel the prophet is expected to hear the word (of judgement) from the Lord, and warn the people to turn from their ways.[11]

References to prophets as watchmen/sentinels are also found in Jeremiah 6.17 ('Also I raised up sentinels for you'); Isaiah 21.11–12 (cf. v. 6) and Hosea 9.8a ('The prophet is a sentinel for my God over Ephraim', cf. 8.1). Although this image is not necessarily widespread, I believe it provides a helpful perspective for understanding the ministry of most of the writing prophets. The role of the pre-exilic prophets was to discern the presence of impending judgement and warn the people of danger. The exilic and post-exilic prophets were also watchmen/sentinels, but in a different sense: instead of watching for impending judgement, they awaited and announced the Deity's imminent work of salvation (cf. Isa. 52.8).

---

[11] The main difference between a standard sentinel and the prophet is that the former is appointed by the people, whereas the latter is appointed by the Lord.

Have you considered?
WERE SOME OF THE WRITING PROPHETS CULT PROPHETS?

When asked to picture a prophet, many people have in mind a solitary figure on the periphery of Israel's society 'despised and rejected by others' (Isa. 53.3) (see Fig. 1.9 overleaf). While such a picture may encapsulate the experience of a number of Israel's writing prophets, it is likely that this was the exception rather than the rule. Instead of existing as solitary, isolated individuals on the fringes of Israel's social and religious life, there is much evidence to suggest that the majority of Israel's prophets would have been located either in one of Israel's sanctuaries or at the royal court. In other words, they were to be found at the heart of Israel's society rather than on its outskirts.

The most likely place to find a prophet in ancient Israel would have been at one of the nation's various sanctuaries, including the Jerusalem Temple. Both writing and non-writing prophets are associated in various ways with Israel's cultic establishments. For example, during the early phase of prophecy in Israel we find prophetic bands or guilds, the 'sons of the prophets' (*běnê haněbî'îm*), living together in or near Israel's major cultic centres such as Bethel (2 Kings 2.3) and Gilgal (2 Kings 4.38) (cf. 1 Sam. 10.5). Given the size and importance of the Jerusalem Temple, it is highly likely that numerous prophets would have been found in or around its precincts.* There is evidence to suggest that some prophets may even have lived within the Temple itself (cf. Jer. 35.4), and most scholars now recognize the existence of specialized cult prophets whose responsibilities probably included the provision of oracles to those who had come to seek the will of Yahweh regarding a significant issue or life problem, and the giving of a word during significant cultic celebrations and gatherings (Lang, 1983: 96).[†]

While it has long been accepted that some of Israel's non-canonical prophets may have had a close association with the cult, the suggestion that some of their canonical counterparts were cult prophets has been a hotly debated topic. Following the work of the Scandinavian scholar Sigmund Mowinckel, however, various scholars have proposed that at least three of the Old Testament writing prophets – Joel, Nahum and Habakkuk – may have been more or less permanently attached to the Jerusalem Temple. What is the evidence for this suggestion? Three features of these books are generally emphasized: the presence of hymnic or liturgical elements within their oracles, the absence of any criticism of the cult and other state institutions, and oracles of salvation against the enemy (Miller, 2000: 176). While it would not necessarily be surprising to discover that one (or more) of these three was closely connected with the Jerusalem cult, Miller's (2000: 176) cautious conclusion that 'the evidence is more suggestive than definitive' seems best.

---

* Texts such as Jer. 23.11 and Lam. 2.20 clearly indicate that the House of the Lord was a hub not only of priestly but also prophetic activity.
[†] Mowinckel identified four psalms (60; 65; 82; 110) which he believed contained examples of prophetic oracles of assurance that would have been delivered within the context of an Israelite worship service.

Figure 1.9 The prophet as a lone and solitary figure; 'The prophet Amos (Amos 1)' from Doré's *English Bible*

Engraving from G. Doré, *The Holy Bible, with Illustrations by Gustave Doré*. London and New York: Cassell, Petter and Galpin, 1866–70. Wikimedia Commons.

1.4 What is a prophetic book?

When readers first encounter the prophetic books it is not uncommon for them to assume that they were written by the prophet whose name appears in the title. Thus, the superscription: 'The words of Amos, who was among the shepherds of Tekoa, which he saw concerning Israel in the days of King Uzziah of Judah and in the days of King Jeroboam son of Joash of Israel, two years before the earthquake' (Amos 1.1) is taken to mean that the prophet Amos is the author of the ensuing material. We need to be aware, however, that this is not exactly what the title claims: while the material is associated with the prophet, the title does not explicitly state that Amos was responsible for writing the words down. The prophets are identified as the recipients of divine revelation, not as literary authors.[12]

---

[12] So, for example, the books do not begin by saying, 'These are the words that the prophet wrote ...' but 'This is the vision the prophet saw ...'.

The actual process by which the (largely spoken) words of the prophets became the written books we now have before us is something of a mystery; the prophetic corpus, though extensive, provides very little information regarding the manner of its composition. It would seem reasonable to assume, however, that at a minimum we are dealing with three distinct 'movements':[13]

1 from oral words to written words;
2 from written words to collected words;
3 from collected words to prophetic book.

It needs to be emphasized, however, that the exact compositional process for each prophetic book was unique. While most books probably followed this general outline, each appears to have grown in its own distinctive way.

1.4.1 Movement one: from oral words to written words

It seems likely that the majority of Israel's prophets, especially the early prophets, delivered their oracles orally. The prophets were essentially speakers, not writers.[14] For example, Ezekiel is commissioned to 'go to the house of Israel and *speak* my very words to them' (Ezek. 3.4), Micah is 'filled with power, with the spirit of the LORD, and with justice and might, to *declare* to Jacob his transgression and to Israel his sin' (Mic. 3.8), and the Lord places his word in the *mouth* of Jeremiah (Jer. 1.9).[15]

Following the oral delivery of the oracles, the prophetic word was recorded in written form, a process sometimes referred to as 'inscription'. The reasons for recording these oral words in written form were probably multiple, but two stand out.[16] First, it served as a means of transmitting the prophet's message to a contemporary audience he could not address in person, such as a group of people who lived at a place distant from the prophet. For example, according to Jeremiah 29, the prophet sent a letter to the Babylonian exiles while he remained in Jerusalem. Second, the inscription of the oracle allowed its message to be preserved for future use, in particular, for the instruction and edification of future generations. In both instances, recording an oral word in written form allows the divine communication to address a much larger audience than would otherwise be possible, an audience distant from the prophet in space and/or time.

---

[13] Collins (1993: 16, 24–5) also posits a broadly similar, three-stage process: (i) the 'pre-book phase' which involved the creation, collection and redaction of material, and which began during the pre-exilic period, (ii) the 'book phase' which involved the organization of the available material into a unified work and which took place during the exilic and post-exilic periods, and (iii) the 'revised book phase' which involved the subsequent revision and further editing of the books.

[14] 'The study of ancient Near Eastern prophecy, biblical prophecy included, is based entirely on the testimony of written texts. No modern researcher has ever witnessed an actual performance of a Babylonian or Israelite prophet. Yet if the written records show us one thing, it is that prophets were originally orators rather than writers' (van der Toorn, 2004: 191).

[15] All emphasis in biblical quotations throughout is mine.

[16] These two reasons were originally identified by van der Toorn (2004: 191–202), whose work has shaped my thinking in this paragraph.

Going deeper:
WAS BARUCH A SCRIBE OR DISCIPLE?

Although Baruch is explicitly referred to as a scribe on two occasions (Jer. 36.26, 32), there are a number of factors which suggest he may have been more than simply a paid employee who was responsible for preserving Jeremiah's words in written form (see Fig. 1.10). For example, Baruch becomes involved in the proclamation of Jeremiah's message when the prophet is no longer able to go to the Temple to speak for himself, and appears to experience an emotional response (i.e. sorrow, pain and lack of rest) to the prophetic message similar to that of Jeremiah himself (45.1–5). Hence, Mowvley concludes: 'Whether or not he [i.e. Baruch] is described as a disciple he certainly looks like one' (1979: 62).

Figure 1.10 'Baruch writes Jeremiah's prophecies (Jer. 36)' from Doré's *English Bible*

Engraving from G. Doré, *The Holy Bible, with Illustrations by Gustave Doré*. London and New York: Cassell, Petter and Galpin, 1866–70. Wikimedia Commons.

Various individuals or groups have been associated with this movement from oral to written words. Prophets themselves may have been responsible; occasionally the Lord commands them to write down the divine words. For example, in Isaiah 8.1 the Lord speaks to the prophet and tells him to 'take a large tablet and write on it in common characters', and in 30.8 he is told, 'Go now, write it before them on a tablet, and inscribe it in a book, so that it may be for the time to come as a witness for ever' (cf. Jer. 30.2; Hab. 2.2). Alternatively, a prophet could have employed a scribe to do the writing. We have clear evidence for this in the book of Jeremiah: 'Then Jeremiah called Baruch son of Neriah, and Baruch wrote on a scroll at Jeremiah's dictation all the words of the LORD that he had spoken to him' (36.4). Since this process is a direct result of the Lord commanding Jeremiah to write down the divine words ('In the fourth year of King Jehoiakim son of Josiah of Judah, this word came to Jeremiah from the LORD: Take a scroll and write on it all the words that I have spoken to you against Israel and Judah', Jer. 36.1–2a), we should not simply assume that all the biblical injunctions for a prophet to write down the divine words necessarily entailed the prophet directly doing this; it was acceptable practice for the prophet to utilize a scribe (see Fig. 1.11). Finally, some scholars have argued for the presence of a circle of disciples who followed the prophet and were responsible for

Figure 1.11 Diorite statue of a seated Egyptian scribe with a papyrus scroll
© Janmad / Wikimedia Commons.

writing down the prophet's words, perhaps shortly following his or her death. Isaiah 8.16 is often cited in this context ('Bind up the testimony, seal the teaching among my disciples'); however, the biblical evidence for such groups is far from overwhelming.[17] Mowvley's cautious conclusion would seem to be appropriate:

> We are bound to say that however slight the evidence may be there must have been some people who listened and who realized that their words had the ring of truth and authority about them and so preserved them for the future so that they may be used and re-used later by others. Beyond that we cannot go at the present time. (1979: 63)

It is impossible to know how closely the written words matched the spoken word as we no longer have access to the latter. While it would seem reasonable to assume that the essential message was closely preserved (after all, this had been given to the prophet by God), some minor modifications may have been introduced. Speaking and writing are two different mediums of communication, and the message may have been recast to work more effectively in written form. Furthermore, if the prophet had delivered the oracle some time before, he or she may have had a chance to reflect on its words: this might shape the way the oracle was explained and recorded.

The time elapse involved in this movement from oral delivery to initial written composition was probably relatively short. The ancient Near Eastern evidence (especially from Mari) suggests that prophetic messages were written down very soon after they were uttered. One Mari letter quotes an oracle given three days before, while other reports were sent on the days the prophet spoke (Millard, 2012: 885). Although some biblical passages may point to a longer timeframe (e.g. in Jer. 36 the prophet receives his instruction to write down all the divine words from the days of Josiah (mid-620s BC) to today (605 BC)), we could well suppose that this process took place within the lifetime of the prophet, if not shortly thereafter.

Have you considered?
THE WRITTEN COMPOSITION OF PROPHETIC ORACLES

So far we have focused on a movement from oral to written word; however, it is possible that sometimes the direction was reversed – some oracles may have been originally composed in written form and then delivered orally.

> It would seem that not all prophetic literature emerged out of an oral environment. There is significant evidence of prophetic literature that was written from the outset. There was flux in the oral/written environment. Words that were spoken could be written, and words that were written could be read. (Petersen, 2009: 642)

---

[17] For further discussion of the prophets' disciples, see Lindblom, 1963: 159–65. For a conservative response, see Wood, 1998: 81–4.

Distinguishing between texts which have an oral basis and texts which were originally composed in written form, however, is not a straightforward process. This is due to the fact that oral modes of discourse inevitably influence the production of written texts. In other words, even written texts would have been composed according to traditional (oral) models, and thus can be difficult to differentiate from their purely oral counterparts.

1.4.2 Movement two: from written words to collected words

The second movement involved gathering together the individually transcribed prophetic oracles and grouping them into collections. The prophetic books are essentially anthologies; they represent the compilation of prophetic oracles (and other material) that were originally delivered at different times and places.

The degree of organization, however, can vary considerably. Some sections in the prophetic books appear to be quite disorganized (there is no obvious relationship between the individual oracles) while others appear to be more carefully arranged. In the case of the latter, three key criteria seem to have been important:

1 Sometimes oracles are grouped together on the basis of *thematic considerations*; for example, Jeremiah 21.11—23.8 constitutes a collection of prose and poetic material, all of which centres on the royal house of Judah. Likewise, oracles against foreign nations are often grouped together (e.g. Isa. 13—23; Jer. 46—51; Ezek. 25—32).
2 In other instances, *chronological considerations* seem to have been primary – the oracles are recorded according to their date of delivery. This approach is particularly noticeable in a book like Haggai.
3 Sometimes *key words or phrases* (catchwords) are used to link together two or more oracles or blocks of material – this process is discernible in a passage such as Amos 7.1—8.3. Here we encounter a series of four vision reports, introduced by the phrase: 'This is what the Lord GOD / he showed me …' (7.1, 4, 7; 8.1). Between the third and fourth vision report, a narrative recording the confrontation between Amos and the priest Amaziah at Bethel has been inserted (7.10–17). The inclusion of this apparently anomalous block of material can be explained on the basis of the presence of a number of catchwords including 'Jeroboam' (Amos 7.9, 10), 'Isaac' (7. 9, 16) and 'plumb-line / [measuring] line' (7.7–8, 17).

As part of this movement, the oracles may have undergone a process of redaction, which involved the material being supplemented or adapted in some way, perhaps to clarify the prophet's message, to bring it up to date, or to apply it to a new context (i.e. to 'recontextualize' it). This process could have begun with the prophet. Petersen (2009: 642) has highlighted Isaiah

15 and 16 as an example of prophetic supplementation. Isaiah 15.1—16.12 contains a speech (or series of speeches) which focuses on the nation of Moab. This is followed by a much shorter, final oracle (16.14b). The bridge between these two sections is found in verses 13–14a: 'This was the word that the LORD spoke concerning Moab in the past. But now the LORD says ...'. What has been said earlier by the prophet now needs to be cast in a new light through the addition of new material.[18] This process may have been continued by others, such as the prophet's disciples or later scribes. For example, the material we find in Isaiah 40—66 appears to supplement the (earlier) material of Isaiah 1—39, with critical scholars arguing that the former stems from a different hand (a prophet or group of prophets who were active during the sixth to fifth centuries) from the latter.

In addition to supplementation (i.e. the addition of new oracles to pre-existing material), some of the prophetic material itself may have been reworked in the process of transmission. A desire to keep the prophet's message alive from one generation to the next may have led to a process of recontextualization. This involved adapting the prophetic material to meet the needs and questions of later times and different circumstances as the transmitters looked to the prophet's divinely inspired words for answers to the predicaments of their own day (Rofé, 1997: 40). Such a process can perhaps be seen in Hosea 1.2–9. This narrative records God's commission to Hosea to marry and produce children that bear names which proclaim the Lord's response to the northern kingdom's (Israel's) unfaithfulness. Verse 7 interrupts the narrative by shifting the focus to Judah and by introducing a word of salvation, which runs counter to the dominant note of judgement sounded throughout the rest of the passage. Some scholars view this as a later, but still pre-exilic, addition, which helps to explain Judah's continued existence even following the loss of the north in 721 BC. Of course, it is not always easy to spot such editorial activity because editors ideally leave little trace of their presence: any material they add is carefully interwoven with what already exists, and any 'touching up' is carefully blended in with the old.

Have you considered?
PROPHETIC PLAGIARISM

Students who have been drilled in the importance of referencing and the appropriate use of sources sometimes raise the issue of plagiarism when it comes to discussing the presence of multiple hands in the composition of prophetic books.

---

[18] This process of prophetic supplementation may also be implied in a passage such as Jer. 36.32 which acknowledges that in Jeremiah's second scroll, his scribe, Baruch, 'wrote on it at Jeremiah's dictation all the words of the scroll that King Jehoiakim of Judah had burned in the fire; *and many similar words were added to them.*'

They initially struggle to reconcile modern conceptions of authorship and composition with ancient practice. In this context, Redditt's discussion is worth quoting in full. He argues that we should not use the language of plagiarism in relation to the prophetic books because

> it brings a modern, idealized concept of authorship to bear on ancient authorship. Apparently people were not concerned much about plagiarism until books could be mass produced by printing, so that authors could earn money from their intellectual output. In modern times to 'steal' someone's words could amount to stealing some of that person's income or at least reputation. Hence, in today's world plagiarism is not only considered unethical, but also illegal. In the ancient world no such prohibitions applied to the work of writers. Besides, there is a real sense in which what they were doing was the opposite of plagiarism. In plagiarism one passes off the work of another author as one's own; in ancient prophecy the later prophets/redactors/scribes were attributing their work to someone else. They were more comparable to ghost writers or presidential speech writers than deceivers. (2008: 16)

1.4.3 Movement three: from collected words to prophetic book

The final stage of composition involved bringing the various collections together and shaping the material into the form which we now have today. A basic pattern of judgement against Israel, judgement of the nations, consolation and restoration of Israel apparently functioned as an organizing principle in a number of cases (e.g. Ezekiel; Isa. 1—39; Jeremiah LXX; Joel;[19] Zephaniah). Introductory superscriptions, which sought to ground the book in a specific historical moment and with a specific historical personage, were added, as were epilogues. Both of these appear to come from a later hand; the superscriptions, for example, often stand out from the main body of the work and speak about the prophet in the third person (in contrast to the oracles themselves where the prophet usually speaks in the first person).

Traditionally, evangelicals (particularly in North America) have argued for a relatively quick compositional process, maintaining that the various books probably reached their final form (or a version very close version to this) during the prophet's lifetime or shortly thereafter. Bullock's statement is representative of this position: 'But it is unlikely that more than a generation intervened between the life of the prophet and the final edition of his book' (2007: 42). They have also stressed that the final redactor was a close associate of the prophet.

Critical scholars, however, have argued for a longer and more complex process, suggesting that the various books probably did not reach their final form until centuries after the lifetime of the named prophet. Rofé, for

---

[19] Joel adds an initial consolation (2.18—3.5) before the oracles against the nations (Joel 4.1–17).

example, suggests that the redactors who were responsible for gathering together the bulk of the prophetic literature 'were active during a fairly late period, somewhere toward the end of the Persian era' (1997: 42). Editing was probably undertaken by a number of different individuals, most of whom had no direct connection with the prophet at all.

Going deeper:
THE BOOK OF JEREMIAH AND THE REDACTION PROCESS

The book of Jeremiah may provide insight into the redactional process the prophetic books underwent. This book has come down to us today in two different versions: the first is the form preserved in the Hebrew Masoretic Text (MT) (and which is the basis for the English-language translation we have in our Bibles); the second has been preserved in the Greek Septuagint (LXX). There are significant differences between the two: the Greek is approximately one-eighth shorter than the Hebrew and after 25.13a the order of materials differs noticeably.

While some scholars have suggested that the differences between the two versions are a result of the work of the Greek translator(s), it now seems more likely that the vast majority of differences are due to the fact that the Greek translator(s) was working from a different, shorter and probably earlier Hebrew text. The longer form, which is reflected in the Masoretic Text, appears to contain a number of later, editorial additions. For example, Jeremiah 25.14; 27.7 seem to be post-exilic additions 'dealing with the punishment of Babylon after seventy years, an issue of interpretation surfacing in several other texts related to this period (2 Chron 36; Ezra 1; Dan 9)' (Stromberg, 2012: 272). Likewise, in Jeremiah 28.16 the prophet announces the Lord's judgement against the false prophet Hananiah, declaring, 'Within this year you will be dead'. The MT, however, adds a short concluding clause which is not present in the LXX version: '. . . because you [i.e. the prophet Hananiah] have spoken rebellion against the LORD.'

> That addition provides a rationale or explanation for why Hananiah must die. Such a rationale prevents Jeremiah from appearing as a vituperative prophet. Instead, he is simply conveying God's message to Hananiah. The addition is clearly designed to present Jeremiah in the best possible light.   (Petersen, 2009: 642)

The example of Jeremiah suggests that redactional activity may have continued long after the death of the prophet. In this instance, it appears that minor adjustments to the text continued to be made well into the post-exilic period, up to 200 years after the prophet's lifetime.

Throughout the late nineteenth and twentieth centuries the evangelical and critical scholarly positions stood in considerable tension with one another, with the book of Isaiah a key battleground. Mainstream critical scholarship tended to identify (at least) two distinct sections within the book: Isaiah 1—39 which was largely attributed to the eighth-century BC prophet sometimes referred to as 'Isaiah of Jerusalem' and 40—66 which was viewed as the work of an unnamed prophet or prophets living during the time of the Babylonian exile (mid- to late sixth century BC) or shortly thereafter. Conservatives, on the other hand, argued that the whole book had to be the work of Isaiah of Jerusalem and that a denial of Isaianic authorship of the second half was essentially a denial of the veracity of the Bible as Jesus himself had quoted from these chapters and referred to the author as Isaiah.

Going deeper:
THE LOCUS OF INSPIRATION

Part of the reason why evangelicals have argued for a relatively fast compositional process is their emphasis on the prophet as the individual inspired by God. Identifying the locus of inspiration with the prophet, however, may be potentially problematic if one believes that sections of the book postdate the prophet's lifetime. If it is the prophet who is inspired, and these sections do not come from the prophet, how then are we to view this material? Perhaps a more satisfactory approach, therefore, is to identify the locus of inspiration in the book itself (i.e. to argue that it is the book and not the prophet which is inspired). Such a view would see God's hand at work throughout the entire compositional process and the various individuals involved with this, guiding the book to its present completed form.

At the end of the day, there is still much we do not know about the composition of the prophetic books: we are not exactly sure who was involved in this process (apart from the prophet) or how long it took. In my opinion, however, our lack of knowledge should not be a cause for concern. Given that it is the biblical text itself that was canonized, our *primary* focus should be on exegeting the text in its final, completed form, rather than trying to explain the exact process by which this came into being. Furthermore, being able to identify the precise historical context of a specific text may make little difference for those exegetes who are particularly concerned with identifying the theological message and witness of the text. For example, locating a passage such as Amos 9.11–15 in the eighth or sixth or fifth century does not greatly impinge on one's understanding of the theological message of the text: the Lord promises that he will restore David's kingdom and bless the people abundantly. Thus, while analysing the process of composition is absolutely essential for understanding how the text reached its final form, this is only the first, introductory step in a larger endeavour: explicating the meaning of the text which now lies before us.

1.5 Summary

Going deeper:
HOW WERE THE PROPHETS DIFFERENT FROM THE PRIESTS?

It is incorrect and potentially unhelpful to draw a hard and fast distinction between Israel's prophets and priests: both Ezekiel and Jeremiah came from priestly families (in fact, Ezekiel is explicitly referred to as a priest, Ezek. 1.3), and both priests and prophets could perform similar roles (e.g. both are expected to intercede for the people). The two offices, however, are usually distinguished on the basis of admission: the priestly office was hereditary (in other words you had to come from a priestly line – you were born a priest), whereas a prophet was called by God.*

Another key difference was the way they received divine revelation: both priests and prophets were expected to be able to identify the will of the Lord (a process commonly referred to as 'divination' in the scholarly literature) and communicate this to the Israelite people, but the way in which they discerned the Lord's will (i.e. practised divination) was different. Essentially, the pre-exilic priests utilized a form of *deductive* or *instrumental* divination: they sought to discern the will of God through the observation of material objects such as the ephod or Urim and Thummim. The prophets, on the other hand, practised *intuitive, mediated* or *inspired* divination: in this case the will of the Lord was revealed directly, usually via a dream, vision or oral communication.[†]

---

* I have questioned this distinction; see Chalmers, 2012: 54.
† For further discussion see Leclerc, 2007: 27–9.

Fundamentally, a prophet was an intermediary: he or she was called to stand between the divine and human realms. Like Israel's priests, the prophets occupied the liminal zone between God and the people; they were members both of the nation of Israel and of the divine council.[20] The prophets' intermediary status is perhaps best illustrated by their role as communicators of the divine will. On one hand, the prophets could be commissioned directly by God to speak a word of judgement or salvation to the people. On the other hand, they could be sought out by people who required divine guidance for a specific issue or problem or divine intervention in a time of crisis. A prophetic book is the written record of the divine revelation mediated to the people of God through the prophet. This revelation addressed the prophet's original audience and the crises they faced; it addressed subsequent audiences (as suggested by attempts to apply the prophet's oracles to new contexts); and it continues to address the people of God today.

---

[20] For further discussion about priests in ancient Israel, see Chalmers, 2012: 15–38.

Further reading

On prophets

Blenkinsopp, J. *Sage, Priest, Prophet: Religious and Intellectual Leadership in Ancient Israel*, LAI. Louisville: WJKP, 1995.

Grabbe, L. *Priests, Prophets, Diviners, Sages: A Socio-Historical Study of Religious Specialists in Ancient Israel*. Valley Forge: Trinity Press, 1995.

Hutton, R. *Charisma and Authority in Israelite Society*. Minneapolis: Fortress, 1994.

Lang, B. *Monotheism and the Prophetic Minority: An Essay in Biblical History and Sociology*, SWBAS 1. Sheffield: Almond Press, 1983.

Matthews, V. *The Hebrew Prophets and Their Social World: An Introduction*, 2nd edn. Grand Rapids: Baker, 2012.

On prophetic books

Collins, T. *The Mantle of Elijah: The Redaction Criticism of the Prophetical Books*, BS 20. Sheffield: JSOT Press, 1993.

Rofé, A. *Introduction to the Prophetic Literature*, BS 21. Sheffield: Sheffield Academic Press, 1997.

Troxel, R. *Prophetic Literature: From Oracles to Books*. Chichester: Wiley-Blackwell, 2012.

2

The historical world of the prophets

2.1 Introduction

The necessity of consulting the historical world of a prophetic text becomes clear when we consider a few sample passages:[1]

> The inhabitants of Samaria tremble
>> for the calf of Beth-aven.
> Its people shall mourn for it,
>> and its idolatrous priests shall wail over it,
>> over its glory that has departed from it.
> The thing itself shall be carried to Assyria
>> as tribute to the great king.
> Ephraim shall be put to shame,
>> and Israel shall be ashamed of his idol.
>
> (Hos. 10.5–6)

> Hear this word, you cows of Bashan
>> who are on Mount Samaria,
> who oppress the poor, who crush the needy,
>> who say to their husbands, 'Bring something to drink!'
> The Lord GOD has sworn by his holiness:
>> The time is surely coming upon you,
> when they shall take you away with hooks,
>> even the last of you with fish-hooks.
> Through breaches in the wall you shall leave,
>> each one straight ahead;
>> and you shall be flung out into Harmon,
>>> says the LORD.
>
> (Amos 4.1–3)

> I will stretch out my hand against Judah,
>> and against all the inhabitants of Jerusalem;
> and I will cut off from this place every remnant of Baal
>> and the name of the idolatrous priests;
> those who bow down on the roofs
>> to the host of the heavens;

---

[1] I use 'historical' here in a broad sense to refer to the world in which the text was produced and first read or heard. Thus, consideration of a text's historical world involves an appreciation of its social, economic, political and religious contexts. This is sometimes referred to as the 'world behind the text'.

those who bow down and swear to the LORD,
  but also swear by Milcom;
those who have turned back from following the LORD,
  who have not sought the LORD or inquired of him.
(Zeph. 1.4–6)

Such passages can leave modern readers with all sorts of questions: what is the calf of Beth-aven? Who is the great king? What or who are the cows of Bashan? Where is Harmon and what is its significance? Who are Baal, the host of the heavens and Milcom? These questions are a consequence of the fact that the prophet expected his audience to understand implicitly the meaning and significance of these words or phrases and thus did not feel the need to explain them. In other words, the prophet assumed that his audience possessed a certain body of knowledge that would allow them to grasp what he was trying to say. Hosea, for example, knew that his audience would recognize that the 'calf of Beth-aven' was in fact a derogatory reference to the idolatrous golden calf which had been set up by Jeroboam I in the sanctuary at Bethel following the division of the kingdom in the tenth century (Beth-aven, which means 'house of wickedness', is a wordplay on Bethel, which means 'house of God'). Amos could be confident that his 'cows of Bashan' would have been understood by his audience as a reference to the privileged, wealthy, upper-class women of Samaria. Similarly, Zephaniah must have felt certain that his audience would know that Baal, the host of the heavens and Milcom were all names of foreign gods, gods whom the Israelites should not have been worshipping. Unfortunately for us, however, a span of more than 25 centuries separates the modern reader from the world of the prophets, and such 'assumed knowledge' is no longer common. Thus, some form of historical research is required if we wish to grasp more fully the message of the various prophets; the kind of research where we attempt to hear and appreciate these passages as their original audience would have.

But the need for historical research is not only created by the fact that we live in a time and place far removed from the prophets. It is also due to the very nature of the prophetic writings themselves – they are occasional litera-ture. To say that the prophets are 'occasional literature' is essentially to suggest that the prophetic utterances were brought forth by specific occasions in Israel's history and were designed to address concrete situations in the life of God's people (usually, but not limited to, religious crises). To put it another way, the prophetic texts are not universal, abstract statements of timeless truth, nor are they predictions of the far distant future. They were written by real people, living in specific historical contexts, to address the particular needs of a certain community (Gorman, 2001: 65). In this context it is worth remind-ing ourselves of the statistics from Fee and Stuart quoted in Chapter 1: 'Less than 2 percent of Old Testament prophecy is messianic. Less than 5 percent specifically describes the new-covenant age. Less than 1 percent concerns events yet to come in our time' (2003: 182). This means that the *vast* majority of

Old Testament prophecy (more than 92 per cent!) addresses either Israel's immediate or imminent situation. If we want to understand the prophetic writings, we need to appreciate their historical context.

In what follows, I will present Israel's history in broad outline from the start of the eighth century through to the middle of the fifth century BC. This should give some idea of the historical context of the various prophets and where and how they fit in Israel's story. In order to structure the discussion, I have subdivided this period of Israel's history into three key phases. These are demarcated by a number of significant events in Israel's history: the fall of the northern kingdom of Israel (c.722 BC), the fall of the southern kingdom of Judah (c.586 BC) and the end of classical prophecy with Malachi (c. mid-fifth century BC). Although we will be primarily concerned with the situation within Israel during these three and a half centuries, it is impossible to appreciate much of what happens without reference to larger, geopolitical changes in the ancient Near East; developments within Egypt and the Mesopotamian empires of Assyria and Babylonia, for example, decisively impact and shape the course of Israel's history. Without some knowledge of these events and developments it is exceedingly difficult to understand the prophetic books. As Fee and Stuart conclude:

> The prophets speak in large measure directly to these events. Unless you know these events, and others within this era too numerous to mention here, you probably will not be able to follow very well what the prophets are saying. God spoke in history and about history. To understand His Word we must know something of that history. (2003: 191–2)

Before we discuss the historical world of Israel's prophets, however, I need to acknowledge two potential difficulties.[2] The first is that the historical context of a prophetic book may not be clear. Perhaps the best example of this reality is Joel. This book lacks concrete indications of its time of composition and details about its author, and thus dates of composition ranging from 800 to 300 BC have been proposed. Where such difficulties exist, I have utilized the dating which I believe has the most scholarly support. The second challenge is that a single book may address multiple historical contexts. For example, it is commonly suggested in critical circles that the book of Isaiah has three distinct historical horizons: pre-exilic (c. late eighth to early seventh century) often referred to as Proto-Isaiah and consisting of most of chapters 1—39; exilic (c.550–539) often referred to as Deutero-Isaiah and consisting

---

[2] There is a third potential difficulty. Some of the prophetic books, especially those originally addressed to the northern kingdom of Israel (i.e. Amos and Hosea), may have been 'updated' or reworked in order to speak into the situation of the people at a later stage, e.g. the southern kingdom following the fall of the north. (For further discussion of the redaction of the prophetic books, see Chapter 1.) These books thus possess an original historical context and a later, redactional one. Such considerations, however, introduce a level of complexity which is beyond the scope of an introductory work such as this and thus I would encourage the interested reader to pursue more detailed discussions in commentaries or monographs.

of chapters 40—55; and post-exilic (c. late sixth to early fifth century) often referred to as Trito-Isaiah and consisting of chapters 56—66.[3] I have attempted to include some consideration of such proposals in the following discussion, even though not all scholars (especially evangelicals) are convinced of their cogency.

2.2 From the start of the eighth century to the fall of the northern kingdom (c.722 BC)

Table 2.1 Key players, events and prophets, 800–722 BC

Time	Key players	Key events and developments	Prophets
800–722 BC	Jeroboam II, king of Israel Uzziah, king of Judah Ahaz, king of Judah Tiglath-Pileser III, king of Assyria Shalmaneser V, king of Assyria	Prosperity of Israel and Judah during the early to mid-eighth century Syro-Ephraimite War Loss of the north to the Assyrian Empire	Amos (Israel) Hosea (Israel) Isaiah of Jerusalem (Judah) Micah (Judah)

Going deeper:
WHY WERE THE ASSYRIANS SO SUCCESSFUL?

Three key factors contributed to Assyria's military success. Unlike the military forces put into the field by smaller nations (such as Israel and Judah), the Assyrians possessed a highly organized standing army which did not have to return home at regular intervals to bring in the crops (Blenkinsopp, 1996: 67). From a techno-logical perspective, the Assyrians were more advanced than their opponents, especially when it came to siege warfare (see Fig. 2.1 overleaf). Finally, the Assy-rians regularly engaged in psychological warfare, using a variety of tactics, including atrocities against civilian populations, as a means of disheartening their opponents. The fear which the Assyrians provoked in their enemies may partially help to explain the reluctance of the prophet Jonah to travel to Nineveh, one of the major cities of the Assyrian Empire.

---

[3] Critical scholars have also argued for the presence of a First and Second Zechariah (chs 1—8 and 9—14 respectively), locating the former in the early post-exilic (or Persian) period and the latter in the Hellenistic. The evidence for this, however, is less compelling. Based on his analysis of recent scholarship, Boda concludes that we should view the book as 'arising from a single stream of prophetic tradition in the Persian period' (2009: 967).

Figure 2.1 The Assyrians besiege a city. Note the three people impaled on stakes in the background

Goodyear, W. *A History of Art: For Classes, Art-Students, and Tourists in Europe.* New York: A. S. Barnes & Company, 1889.

At the start of the eighth century BC (see Table 2.1 on the previous page), Assyria was the dominant superpower of the ancient Near East. Assyria's heartland was located in northern Mesopotamia, but a series of strong kings, including Ashurnasirpal II (883–859), Shalmaneser III (858–823) and Adad-nirari III (810–782), had extended the empire's boundaries from the Caspian to the Mediterranean Sea (see Fig. 2.2). During the first half of the eighth century, however, the empire experienced a short period of weakness. Facing internal revolts and serious plagues, Assyria's immediate interest in the region of Syria-Palestine was diminished.

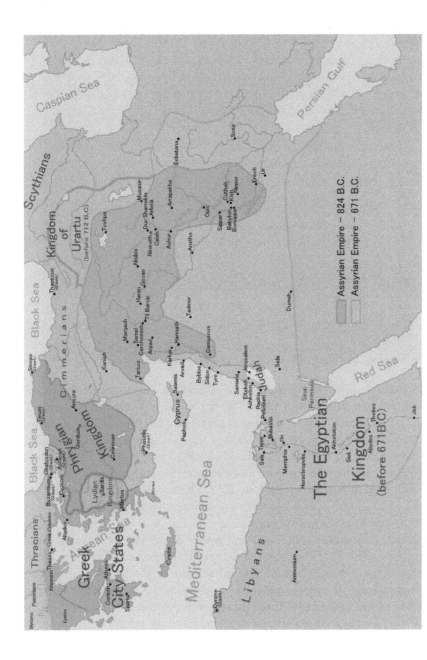

Figure 2.2 Map of the Assyrian Empire

Archaeological insight:
THE PROSPERITY OF THE NORTHERN KINGDOM

Archaeological evidence for the prosperity of the northern kingdom is provided by fragments of carved ivory found in the capital, Samaria, which were used to decorate walls and furniture (see Fig. 2.3). Ivory was an expensive commodity, and its presence points to the wealth and affluence of the ruling class in contrast to the subsistence-level existence of most of the population, who lived off the land (Blenkinsopp, 1996: 71). Amos' critique of the owners of such items is harsh:

> Alas for those who lie on beds of ivory,
>   and lounge on their couches,
> and eat lambs from the flock,
>   and calves from the stall;
> who sing idle songs to the sound of the harp,
>   and like David improvise on instruments of music;
> who drink wine from bowls,
>   and anoint themselves with the finest oils,
>   but are not grieved over the ruin of Joseph!
> Therefore they shall now be the first to go into exile,
>   and the revelry of the loungers shall pass away.
> (Amos 6.4–7; cf. 3.13–15)

These ivories also point to the cosmopolitan nature of the northern kingdom's capital as they exhibit strong Egyptian, Syrian and Phoenician artistic influences.

The weakness of Assyria proved to be a positive development for Israel. The northern king Jeroboam II (786–746 BC) was able to expand his borders, restoring Israelite territory in the north and east (2 Kings 14.25; cf. Amos 6.13–14). Chronicles suggest that Jeroboam's southern counterpart, King Uzziah (aka Azariah), was able to rebuild the Red Sea port of Elath, defeat the Philistines, secure the Negeb, exact tribute from the Ammonites, and fortify and arm Jerusalem (2 Chron. 26).[4] These developments appear to have had significant socio-economic implications, with both the biblical text and archaeological record suggesting that this was an epoch of urban development, expanding trade and increased availability of luxury items (Blenkinsopp, 1996: 71). The material prosperity of the urban upper classes, however, was bought with a price; the inhabitants of the towns and villages of the countryside (in other words, the majority of the population) suffered increased hardship in order to 'fund' these developments. It is into this situation that the prophet **Amos** speaks, fiercely attacking what he perceives to be the widespread social injustice of the time, including the exploitation of the poor and corrupt legal practices (see Fig. 2.4 overleaf).

---

[4] The book of Kings tells us little about Uzziah/Azariah apart from the fact that he had a long reign (52 years), 'did what was right in the sight of the LORD' and suffered from a skin condition (2 Kings 15.1–7).

Figure 2.3 Some of the ivories from Samaria

Courtesy William Dever. Based on plates from J. Crowfoot and G. Crowfoot, *Early Ivories from Samaria*,
London: Palestine Exploration Fund, 1938.

Figure 2.4 The Assyrian royal couple, Ashurbanipal and his queen, reclining on couches and drinking from bowls. They are attended by eight servants, including a musician with a harp and another with a cone-shaped drum. The description of 'those who lie on beds of ivory' in Amos 6 matches closely this portrayal of the Assyrian monarch

Hall, H. *Babylonian and Assyrian Sculpture in the British Museum*. Paris: Les Éditions G. van Oest, 1928.

Going deeper:
A SOCIOLOGICAL ANALYSIS OF ISRAELITE SOCIETY IN THE TIME OF JEROBOAM II

The proposal of sociologists that Israelite society in the time of Jeroboam II and his successors be analyzed as an 'advanced agrarian society' is convincing. The principle of patrimonial inheritance had largely given way to a system in which gifts (prebends) of land from the throne had produced estates held by people who lived most of the time at the court. As part of the same development, lands in the hands of common folk were acquired by the large landowners when small landholders could no longer survive economically. A system of 'rent capitalism' is likely to have come into play whereby the landed peasantry had to sell land in bad seasons in order to buy seed to plant what land they retained, and a cycle began that ended in peasantry operating as tenant farmers, owing their livelihood to their patrons. An economic elite came to possess most of the land; more and more people became landless. In the midst would have been people of commerce, who traded in necessities like tools and seed, as well as in luxury items.   (Campbell, 1998: 234–5)

Archaeological insight:
THE SAMARIA OSTRACA

The Samaria Ostraca consist of over 100 inscribed potsherds (broken pieces of pottery) which are dated to the eighth century BC (probably during the reign of Jeroboam II) and were discovered in the capital of the northern kingdom. These short texts are receipts which record the delivery of wine or oil, with each containing at least one personal name. A significant number of these names include a Baal element within them (e.g. Meriba'al, Abiba'al), suggesting that the worship of this god was quite common in the north.

Figure 2.5 'She did not know that it was I who gave her the grain, the wine, and the oil, and who lavished upon her silver and gold that they used for Baal' (Hos. 2.8). Limestone stele from Ugarit depicting Baal with thunderbolt

© Marie-Lan Nguyen / Wikimedia Commons.

The religious situation of the northern kingdom, in particular, was also problematic. **Hosea** suggests that unfaithfulness towards Yahweh, manifested, for example, in worship of the Canaanite storm god Baal, was widespread (Hos. 2.8; 13.1) (see Fig. 2.5), an assertion which would seem to be supported by the presence of names with a Baal theophoric element in the Samaria Ostraca (see box on p. 42).[5] The idolatrous sanctuaries at Dan and

---

[5] For more details about the worship of Baal in ancient Israel, see Chalmers, 2012: 106–7.

Bethel continued to draw worshippers, while the religious ceremonies of the people appear to have been superficial, with little impact on their everyday lives or how they treated their neighbour (Amos 5.10–12, 21–24; 8.4–8). Thus both Amos and Hosea announce God's intention to act in judgement against the northern kingdom of Israel.

Following the death of Jeroboam II (746 BC), the situation of the northern kingdom rapidly deteriorated. Internally, the kingdom experienced a period of significant political instability, with five kings (three of whom were assassinated) ruling in a space of 23 years. Externally, a reinvigorated Assyria under the leadership of a new king, Tiglath-Pileser III, who had come to the throne in 745 BC, began to pose a renewed threat.[6] Keen to flex his empire's muscles, Tiglath-Pileser embarked on a period of rapid military expansion, solidifying his hold over the territories previously held by Adad-nirari III.

From 738 BC onwards the Assyrians made a series of incursions into Israel, reducing the northern kingdom to vassalage and imposing a heavy tribute (cf. 2 Kings 15.19–20). Particularly important for the prophets were the events of 735/4. In an ill-fated attempt to secure their independence, the northern kingdom of Israel (under King Pekah) entered into an alliance with Syria (under King Rezin). Judah, however, refused to participate, and in response the combined armies of Israel and Syria invaded the southern kingdom as a means of forcing the nation's hand. These events, commonly referred to as the Syro-Ephraimite War ('Ephraim' is a title for the northern kingdom commonly employed in Hebrew poetry), form the background for a number of prophetic passages, including Isaiah 7—8 and Hosea 5.8–14; 8.7–10. In a desperate move (and against the advice of the prophet Isaiah), King Ahaz of Judah appealed to Tiglath-Pileser III for assistance. The Assyrian king responded by attacking Israel and Syria, capturing portions of their territory, including Damascus, the capital of Syria. Tiglath-Pileser's intervention relieved Judah of its immediate threat but ensured the nation's status as an Assyrian vassal (cf. 2 Kings 16.7). This development seems to have impacted the nation politically and religiously, with Ahaz embracing foreign traditions. We are told, for example, that Ahaz had an altar erected in the Jerusalem Temple which was modelled after one he had seen in Damascus during his audience with Tiglath-Pileser (2 Kings 16.10–18).

Following the death of Tiglath-Pileser III in 727, the northern Israelite kingdom again attempted to rebel against its Assyrian overlords. After securing his position, Tiglath-Pileser's son, Shalmaneser V, invaded the northern kingdom repeatedly, eventually capturing the capital, Samaria, in 722 BC. A significant portion of the leading citizens of the nation (27,290 according to the Assyrian records), including the aristocracy, soldiers and artisans, were

---

[6] Tiglath-Pileser III is referred to by his alternative name, Pul, in 2 Kings 15.19.

taken into exile, and people from other areas of the Assyrian Empire were shipped in in their place. This event is usually taken to mark the end of the northern kingdom.[7] The prophetic warnings of Amos and Hosea had been fulfilled.

Going deeper:
WHY DID THE ASSYRIANS PRACTISE DEPORTATION?

The practice of deportation provided a number of potential benefits in terms of securing and strengthening the heartland of the Assyrian Empire. First of all, it separated the conquered from their homelands (see Fig. 2.6), thereby diminishing the likelihood of nationalistic uprisings (Coogan, 2010: 309).* The resettled population also provided a ready-made labour force and could be involved in establishing new cities, and rebuilding ones which had fallen into ruins. Soldiers were conscripted into the Assyrian army while those skilled in farming could be used to cultivate previously undeveloped regions, thereby adding to the agricultural productivity of the empire.

---

* It was believed that those who were resettled, particularly in potentially dangerous border areas, would realize that their safety and well-being depended on the Assyrians, and therefore were more likely to be loyal (Gowan, 1998: 13).

Figure 2.6 The aftermath of conquest. The inhabitants of the city, women and children, are being carried away in carts drawn by teams of oxen

Hall, H. *Babylonian and Assyrian Sculpture in the British Museum.* Paris: Les Éditions G. van Oest, 1928.

---

[7] Following the loss of the northern kingdom, the title 'Israel' can be applied to the south (Judah).

2.3 From the fall of the northern kingdom to the fall of the southern kingdom (c.586 BC)

The south continued to exist as a semi-independent kingdom following the fall of the north (see Table 2.2). There was still a Davidic king on the throne, but the nation remained largely subject to Assyria. Internal problems, especially social injustice, continued to plague the kingdom, and the prophets **Isaiah** and **Micah** warned the nation's political and religious leaders that if they did not turn from their oppressive ways, they would suffer the same fate as the north: invasion and destruction by a foreign power. Micah's preaching seems to have been particularly effective (see Fig. 2.7). Hezekiah (who had come to the throne in 715 BC) was won over by the prophet's dire predictions of

Figure 2.7 'Micah exhorts the Israelites to repent (Mic. 7)' from Doré's *English Bible*

Engraving from G. Doré, *The Holy Bible, with Illustrations by Gustave Doré*. London and New York: Cassell, Petter and Galpin, 1866–70. Wikimedia Commons.

Table 2.2 Key players, events and prophets, 722–586 BC

Time	Key players	Key events and developments	Prophets
722–586 BC	Hezekiah, king of Judah Manasseh, king of Judah Josiah, king of Judah Jehoiakim, king of Judah Zedekiah, king of Judah Sennacherib, king of Assyria Neco II, king of Egypt Nabopolassar, king of Babylon Nebuchadnezzar, king of Babylon	Religious reforms of Hezekiah and Josiah Assyrian invasion of Judah (701) Apostasy under Manasseh Defeat of the Assyrians at Carchemish Capture of Jerusalem by the Babylonians (597 and 586)	Micah Isaiah of Jerusalem Zephaniah Jeremiah Nahum Habakkuk Ezekiel Obadiah

Jerusalem's destruction, and the nation was spared, at least for a time (cf. Jer. 26.1–19).

From 705 BC onwards Hezekiah began to distance Judah from the Assyrians, withholding tribute and allying himself with Egypt. This move seems to have been an attempt to capitalize on a short period of instability within the Assyrian Empire. The Assyrian king Sargon II had just died while campaigning in distant Anatolia, and the most pressing problem for his successor, Sennacherib, was to maintain control over a resurgent Babylon.

By 701 BC, however, Sennacherib had consolidated his position, and he could thus turn his attention to Syria-Palestine. He invaded Judah with devastating force, capturing all the major cities (including Lachish), and laid siege to Jerusalem. Hezekiah sought the advice of the prophet Isaiah, who urged the king to trust in the Lord's protection of the city and its Davidic king. Isaiah's counsel was vindicated when the capital was spared, although the precise reasons for this remain unclear. According to Isaiah 36—39 and 2 Kings 18—19, the Angel of the Lord struck down 185,000 men in the Assyrian camp, forcing the besieging army to withdraw. Assyrian records, on the other hand, attribute the withdrawal of their forces to Hezekiah submitting and paying a heavy tribute. Whichever interpretation we follow, it is clear that Judah was not fully incorporated into the Assyrian Empire at this stage, though it continued in vassalage and was reduced in size.[8]

---

[8] Ahlström (1982: 68) suggests that most of the territory of Judah was given over to the Philistines, and only Jerusalem and part of the Judaean desert was left for Hezekiah to rule.

Ancient Near Eastern parallels:
ASSYRIAN VERSIONS OF THE CONQUEST OF JUDAH

The Bible is not the only ancient Near Eastern document to record Sennacherib's invasion of Judah and siege of Jerusalem. Three virtually identical prisms (the Taylor Prism, Sennacherib Prism and Jerusalem Prism) which date from 691 to 689 BC provide the Assyrian version of events. Here Sennacherib proclaims:

> As for Hezekiah, the Judean, I besieged forty-six of his fortified walled cities and surrounding smaller towns, which were without number. Using packed-down ramps and applying battering rams, infantry attacks by mines, breeches, and siege machines, I conquered (them) . . . He himself, I locked up within Jerusalem, his royal city, like a bird in a cage. I surrounded him with earthworks, and made it unthinkable for him to exit by the city gate.   (Cogan in *COS*, vol. 2, 303)

Sennacherib also had a massive relief created for a room in his palace in Nineveh in order to commemorate his military triumphs. This included a depiction of his siege and eventual capture of Lachish, an important Judahite military and administrative centre (see Fig. 2.8).

Figure 2.8 Detail from the Lachish reliefs showing the Assyrian army attacking the gate area of Lachish and people departing from the city

Courtesy David Ussishkin, Tel Aviv University. Artist: Judith Dekel.

The other significant development that took place during Hezekiah's reign was a series of religious reforms. These included the removal of the local cultic sanctuaries (referred to as 'high places'), the destruction of their accoutrements (including the pillars and sacred Asherah-poles) and the smashing of the bronze serpent, Nehushtan, to whom the people had begun making offerings. As a result, Hezekiah is remembered very favourably in the biblical text: 'there was no one like him among all the kings of Judah after him, or among those who were before him' (2 Kings 18.5).

Archaeological insight:
THE ALTAR AT BEER-SHEBA AND HEZEKIAH'S REFORMS

Possible archaeological evidence for the reforms of Hezekiah comes from Tel Beer-Sheba. Here archaeologists uncovered the partial remains of a very large (1.57 metre high) altar which was constructed of ashlar masonry (see Fig. 2.9), and which probably had a horn located on the top of each corner (the horns may have symbolized the strength of the altar). Interestingly, the altar was not found *in situ*. Instead it had been broken down and some of the stones reused in the construction of a storehouse wall. Although we cannot be certain why the altar was decommissioned, it has been suggested that this process may have been connected with Hezekiah's cultic reforms which targeted non-Jerusalemite sanctuaries.

Figure 2.9 The reconstructed altar from Tel Beer-Sheba
© Tamarah Hayardeni / Wikimedia Commons.

While Hezekiah is remembered in the biblical text as a pious king, his son, Manasseh, is portrayed as the exact opposite. Manasseh ruled Judah between 687 and 642 BC and, according to the author of 2 Kings, his reign marked the spiritual low point of the nation.[9] Manasseh sought to undo much of the work of his father: he rebuilt the high places, erected altars for Baal, had an image of the goddess Asherah placed in the Jerusalem Temple, and built altars for and worshipped the host of heaven (perhaps implying an adoption of Assyrian astral religious practices and beliefs). On the broader ancient Near Eastern geopolitical scene, Manasseh appears to have been a loyal subject of Assyria, which was experiencing a period of strength under first Esarhaddon (681–669) and later Ashurbanipal (669–627). Assyrian records even indicate that Manasseh provided materials for the construction of a palace and royal storehouses in the capital of Nineveh as well as troops for the successful Assyrian campaign against Egypt in 667–663 BC.[10] Although there is a distinct lack of recorded prophetic activity from this period (a noticeable feature given its presence both before and after his reign), the brutal silencing of any opposition – 'Manasseh shed very much innocent blood' (2 Kings 21.16) – perhaps implies that this was present. Furthermore, the impact of Manasseh's reign may be seen in the book of **Zephaniah**, even though this is set during the early years of the next king's reign (Josiah). In this work the prophet announces judgement on the corruption, injustice and non-Yahwistic religious practices (cf. 1.4–5) which seem to have characterized Manasseh's time on the throne.

Following the death of Ashurbanipal in 627 BC the Assyrian Empire underwent a rapid decline. Overextended and plagued by civil war, the central government found it increasingly difficult to hold down the subject provinces. These difficulties were only compounded by the re-emergence of powerful enemies, including the Elamites from the Iranian highlands, Scythians from the Caucasus region, and Babylon. Thus, we begin to see a significant weakening of Assyrian influence over the region of Syria-Palestine. It is probably around this time that we can date the book of **Nahum**. This prophet condemns the terrible cruelty and oppression of the Assyrians and announces that the Lord will totally destroy their capital, Nineveh, bringing an end to the Assyrian Empire.

Manasseh's son and the next king of Judah, Josiah (640–609 BC), appears to have resembled his grandfather, Hezekiah, more closely than his father. Around 622 BC Josiah launched his own series of religious reforms designed to rid the country of Canaanite, and possibly Assyrian, religious practices, and centralize worship in Jerusalem. Josiah probably had multiple motivations for these actions. The author of 2 Kings views Josiah's work as a pious response to the discovery and reading of the 'book of the law', traditionally understood in critical scholarship to be a form of the book of Deuteronomy, which was found during Temple repairs (2 Kings 22—23). It is also possible, however, that political considerations were involved, with Josiah attempting to capitalize on

---

[9] In fact, Manasseh's reign is singled out as being largely responsible for the subsequent exile of the nation (cf. 2 Kings 21.10–15).

[10] The Assyrians reached the height of their power when their army captured the Egyptian capital of Thebes in 663 BC. This event is alluded to in Isa. 20.4.

Assyria's growing weakness. In fact, Blenkinsopp (1996: 117) has suggested that the extension of Josiah's reforming activity into the region of the old northern kingdom (2 Kings 23.15–20), an Assyrian province at the time, clearly signalled an intent to throw off the Assyrian yoke. 'Josiah's reforms in the North symbolically made the country fit for the worship of the Lord and may have been intended as a prelude to a political claim that would have reconstituted the old Davidic empire' (Wilson, 1993: 599). **Jeremiah** began his long prophetic ministry either shortly before or during the time of Josiah's reforms.

Going deeper:
THE PROPHETESS HULDAH

Upon hearing the words of 'the book of the law', King Josiah tore his clothes and commanded a group of senior officials (including the high priest Hilkiah) to 'inquire of the LORD for me, for the people, and for all Judah, concerning the words of this book that has been found' (2 Kings 22.13). The officials consulted with the prophetess Huldah who delivered a typical prophetic oracle to them (2 Kings 22.15–20). Unfortunately, the biblical text does not provide much information about Huldah, apart from the fact that she was the wife of Shallum son of Tikvah and resided in Jerusalem's Second Quarter. It would seem reasonable to assume, however, that she was an esteemed and well-known figure within Jerusalemite society, given that she was specifically sought out by such senior figures. Due to the fact that her husband is described as the 'keeper of the wardrobe', and thus may have been a member of the royal court (assuming the reference is to the *king's* wardrobe) or Temple (assuming the reference is to the *high priest's* wardrobe), Huldah has been identified as a court or cult prophet. Such suggestions, however, lack clear textual support.

The weakening and divided Assyrian Empire was ultimately unable to hold down a reinvigorated Babylon under Nabopolassar. In 612 BC the Assyrian capital, Nineveh, fell to the combined forces of the Babylonians and Medes, fulfilling the word of the Lord through the prophet Nahum. The Assyrians then formed an alliance with Egypt in a last-ditch attempt to halt the menacing Babylonian war machine. The Egyptian pharaoh, Neco II, marched north from Egypt in 609 BC to assist his Assyrian allies. Along the way he killed King Josiah at Megiddo, and brought Judah under Egyptian control.

The Egyptians appointed first Jehoahaz (609) and then Jehoiakim (609–598 BC) as king over Judah. Jehoiakim reversed the religious reforms of Josiah, clashing frequently with the prophet **Jeremiah** who was active during his reign (Jer. 22.13–19; 26.1–19). Jeremiah condemned the continual disregard for the covenant demands of justice and righteousness in public life, warning that this would lead to God punishing his people. Politically, Jehoiakim ruled as an Egyptian puppet (which involved collecting the significant annual tribute, cf. 2 Kings 23.35), and such complicity with a foreign power would have made him unpopular with many of the citizens of Judah. It is therefore unsurprising to hear of bloodshed, and the execution of dissidents, including prophets (Jer. 26.20–23), during his reign.

In 605 BC the Babylonians crushed the Assyrians and their Egyptian allies at Carchemish, effectively establishing themselves as the unrivalled superpower of the ancient Near East. The Babylonian army, under King Nebuchadnezzar II, pursued the retreating Egyptian forces to Palestine, bringing Judah into their sphere of influence. Although he had been a loyal Egyptian vassal up to this point, Jehoiakim quickly switched sides, pledging fealty to the Babylonians. In 601 BC, however, the Babylonians attempted to invade Egypt, only to be repulsed at the border. Nebuchadnezzar returned to Babylonia to reorganize his army, prompting Jehoiakim to switch allegiances once more – this time back to the Egyptians.

The reprieve from Babylonian control, however, was only short-lived. By 598 BC Nebuchadnezzar had rebuilt his army and moved against vacillating Judah. Jehoiakim died and his 18-year-old son, Jehoiachin, lacking Egyptian support, quickly surrendered to the Babylonians. Like the Assyrians before them, the Babylonians adopted a policy of forced deportation, exiling the king along with a significant number of the leading citizens of the nation (the author of 2 Kings puts the figure at 10,000, 24.14), one of whom was Ezekiel, to Babylon. At this point, however, the city of Jerusalem itself was largely spared. The book of **Habakkuk** appears to represent a response to the Babylonian invasion of Judah, with the prophet questioning God's justice and how the Lord could raise up a wicked foreign power to punish his people.

A second, more devastating conquest was to follow. An uprising in Babylon in 595 BC led Judah and some of its neighbours (including Edom, Moab, Ammon, Tyre and Sidon) to begin planning an insurrection against their Babylonian overlords. The Judahite king and last of the Davidic dynasty, Zedekiah, had failed to learn from the examples of his predecessors and decided to rebel, a move which would have disastrous consequences for the nation. After regaining total control of Babylonia, Nebuchadnezzar marched south to punish his mutinous subjects. He destroyed Judah's remaining fortresses and cities, and laid siege to Jerusalem. Edom appears to have taken advantage of Judah's troubles at this time, and thus comes in for harsh rebuke in the book of **Obadiah**. In July 586 BC, the Babylonians eventually succeeded in breaking through the walls of Jerusalem, and their vengeance was severe. They plundered and destroyed much of the city, including the Solomonic Temple, killed thousands of Judah's citizens and took most of the survivors into exile. The divine judgement which the prophets had continually warned the nation about had come to pass (see Fig. 2.10).

Figure 2.10 An image of exile from the Lachish reliefs. The top row shows Assyrian soldiers carrying off booty they have captured from the city. The bottom row depicts Judahite prisoners being taken away along with their goods and animals

2.4 From the fall of the southern kingdom to the end of classical prophecy (c.450 BC)

Although 586 BC witnessed the most significant deportation of Judah's population, this was not the last (see Table 2.3). Further forced displacements (the Babylonians again invaded in 582 BC) and population movements occurred, one of which included Jeremiah being taken to Egypt by other Judahites against his will (Jer. 42—44). It is worth emphasizing, however, that not all the citizens were taken into exile; Judah was not an empty land devoid of inhabitants. Some, especially members of the poorer and lower classes, were allowed to remain. The writer of 2 Kings 25.12 suggests that the captain of the Babylonian guard, Nebuzaradan, 'left some of the poorest people of the land to be vine-dressers and tillers of the soil' (cf. Jer. 39.9–10). Life must have been very difficult for those people left behind, especially in the years immediately following the events of 586 BC. There was significant political instability, including the assassination of the Babylonian-appointed governor, Gedaliah, and Lamentations points to widespread famine and hardship (Lam. 4.10 suggests that the situation was so desperate that some mothers ate their own children!). In a significant departure from Assyrian practice, however, the Babylonians did not import foreign people-groups into Judah.

Table 2.3 Key players, events and prophets, 586–450 BC

Time	Key players	Key events and developments	Prophets
586–450 BC	Nebuchadnezzar, king of Babylon	Defeat of the Babylonians by the	Ezekiel Deutero-Isaiah
	Cyrus, king of Persia	Persians	Haggai
	Zerubbabel, governor	Return from exile	Zechariah
	of Yehud	Rebuilding of the	Joel
		Temple	Malachi

Due to a lack of significant, contemporary ancient Near Eastern or biblical evidence, it is hard to gauge what life was like for those taken into exile by the Babylonians. On one level, it appears that their existence was not too difficult. While some of the exiles were employed as forced labour in imperial construction projects, this appears to have been the exception rather than the rule. Most seem to have been encouraged to pursue their trade or work as farmers, contributing to the agricultural productivity of the empire. Others appear to have made a successful career in commerce (see box on p. 55), while the example of Daniel and his fellow young countrymen suggests that Judahites could even rise to significant positions within the Babylonian administration. Unlike the Assyrians before them, the Babylonians allowed the different ethnic groups they had resettled to form their own self-contained communities (cf. Ezek. 1.1–3), thus maintaining their separate identity and keeping alive their historical, legal and cultic traditions (Blenkinsopp, 1996: 149). This may help to explain why the southern tribes survived exile, while those of the north did not.

Archaeological insight:
THE ARCHIVES OF MURASHU

Evidence for the integration of people of Judahite descent into the wider economic life of Babylonian society is provided by the archives of Murashu. These documents, which are dated to the second half of the fifth century BC, include contracts, records and receipts of the trading house of the Murashu family from Nippur, a city near Babylon. Significantly, these business transactions contain references to approximately 80 Jews, suggesting that they were fully engaged in the commercial life of the city, involved in loans, leases and other economic dealings. It needs to be acknowledged, however, that the use of these documents to reconstruct life in the exilic period is open to debate given the fact that they were composed approximately 100 years later and point to conditions under the subsequent, Persian administration.

We need to be careful, however, of glossing over the significant suffering and trauma which would have been raised by the experience of exile. Recent anthropological research has shown that such forced migrations constitute a serious socio-psychological crisis which would have 'forced the deportees into destabilizing recalibrations of their communal and theological understandings' (Moore and Kelle, 2011: 364). The loss of their homeland, the destruction of the Temple, and the physical suffering and psychological terror inflicted by enemy armies must have led to intense theological ferment among the exiles in Babylon as they sought to find meaning in the series of tragedies they had suffered and discern the future of their relationship with Yahweh. It is in this context that we need to understand the message of **Ezekiel**, who ministered to the exiles living in Tel-abib, a town in southern Babylonia, for a period of almost 30 years (592–562 BC). Prior to the destruction of the city of Jerusalem in 586 BC, Ezekiel repeatedly warned those already taken into exile that the city and its Temple were doomed, thereby preparing the people for its imminent loss. Following the fall, however, Ezekiel's message shifted to one of consolation, hope and restoration as he announced a return from exile and the rebuilding of Jerusalem and its Temple.

Nebuchadnezzar ruled the Babylonian Empire, which included vast swathes of the ancient Near East, from 605 to 562 BC (see Fig. 2.11 overleaf). After

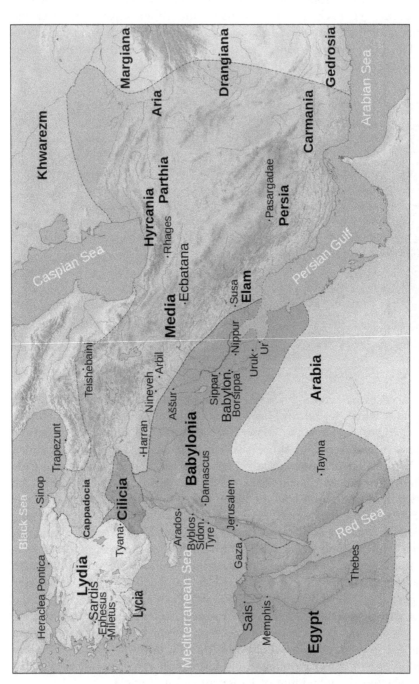

Figure 2.11 Map of Egyptian, Babylonian and Medo-Persian Empires in the sixth century BC

WillemBK's English-language version of a map originally created by Szajci / Wikimedia Commons.

his death, however, Babylonian influence began to wane; he was succeeded by a number of kings (including Nabonidus) who proved to be largely ineffective rulers. Thus **Deutero-Isaiah** proclaimed to the captives in Babylon that the end of their exile was imminent: Israel 'has served her term . . . her penalty is paid' (40.2).[11] The prophet foresaw that Israel's deliverance would be achieved via the arrival of a new world power (the Persians,[12] led by Cyrus the Great[13]) which had been raised up by God to subdue the nations so that Israel might be set free and Jerusalem rebuilt.[14] In 539 BC the Persians captured Babylon and thus, by virtual default, brought Judah into their purview. They would rule the region for the next 200 years.

In 538 BC, one year after conquering Babylon, Cyrus issued a decree stating that the Jews who had been taken into exile could return to their homeland in order to rebuild the Jerusalem Temple (cf. Ezra 1). This begins what is commonly referred to as the post-exilic period, with a series of 'waves' of Jews making the long trek back to Judah (which was now also known by its Persian title Yehud).[15] While many, if not the majority, actually chose to remain in Babylonia (after all, this was the land where they had been born and established themselves, and a run-down backwater like Yehud would have held little attraction[16]), those who did return home saw this as the hand of God at work, and began the long and slow process of rebuilding.

Archaeological insight:
THE CYRUS CYLINDER

The Cyrus Cylinder (see Fig. 2.12 overleaf) was discovered in the ruins of Babylon in 1879 and is currently housed in the British Museum in London. It describes how

---

[11] It needs to be acknowledged that not all scholars recognize the presence of a distinct Deutero-Isaiah, instead attributing the entire book to the eighth-to-seventh-century Isaiah of Jerusalem. It is clear, however, that even if these chapters are not the product of a separate prophetic figure, they are addressing a different historical context (that of exiles who have experienced God's judgement).

[12] The Persians were an Indo-European people who had settled in Parsa, the mountainous land east of the Persian Gulf's northern coastline, by the sixth century BC (Leith, 1998: 283).

[13] The Persians had earlier allied with the Medes, leading some scholars to refer to this as the Medo-Persian Empire.

[14] Cyrus is mentioned in Isa. 44.28; 45.1; 45.13; and Dan. 1.21; 6.28; 10.1. In Isaiah he is given the titles 'shepherd' and 'anointed'. These titles were usually applied to Israel's kings (in fact, Cyrus is the only non-Israelite to be called God's 'anointed').

[15] Yehud was a small province in the large Persian satrapy known as *Aber-Nahara* (which means 'Across the River', that is, across the Euphrates from Persia), which comprised Babylon (until 482), Syria-Palestine (including the coastal Phoenician city-states) and Cyprus.

[16] Babylon was the centre of the known world. Its population at the end of the Neo-Assyrian period (i.e. late seventh century) has been estimated at 120,000 people. The entire population of Judah during the early post-exilic period (late sixth century), on the other hand, was perhaps no more than 10,000 people, and Jerusalem probably had fewer than a thousand residents (Coogan, 2010: 421).

Cyrus was chosen by the Babylonian god Marduk to bring peace and order to his city and to restore the god's cult. Of particular interest for students of the Old Testament is how Cyrus allowed certain people who had been subjugated by the Babylonians to return to their homelands and rebuild their places of worship, suggesting that his activities towards the Jews were part of a wider imperial policy.

> As far as Ashur and Susa, Agade, Eshnunna, the towns of Zamban, Me-Turnu, Der as well as the region of the Gutians, I returned to (these) sacred cities on the other side of the Tigris, the sanctuaries of which have been ruins for a long time, the image which (used) to live therein and established for them permanent sanctuaries. I (also) gathered all their (former) inhabitants and returned (to them) their habitations. Furthermore, I resettled upon the command of Marduk, the great lord, all the gods of Sumer and Akkad whom Nabonidus has brought into Babylon to the anger of the lord of the gods, unharmed, in their (former) chapels, the places which make them happy.
>
> (Oppenheim in *ANET*, 316)

So why did Cyrus choose this course of action? On the surface, this gesture seems to be remarkably magnanimous. We need to realize, however, that there was a (large) degree of self-interest in Cyrus' decision. Such actions would have been well received by the subject populations of the Persian Empire, thereby encouraging their loyalty. This was particularly important for those provinces located on the fringes of the empire (like Judah), who could serve as a buffer with Persia's enemies, such as Egypt. Furthermore, contented vassals would be more likely to accept the regional governors appointed by the Persians whose role included administering the local levies. In other words, any religious piety on Cyrus' part was also tempered by military and economic considerations.

Figure 2.12 The Cyrus Cylinder (British Museum)
Courtesy Gary Stevens / Flickr.

Have you considered?
DID THE TEMPLE REBUILDING HAVE TO START FROM SCRATCH?

On the basis of the description of the Babylonian siege given in 2 Kings 25 it is commonly assumed that the Jerusalem Temple and its altar were completely destroyed. This may not, however, have been the case. In Jeremiah 41.4–7 we hear of 80 worshippers coming to the Temple area after the Babylonian conquest in order to offer grain offerings and incense, perhaps suggesting that part of the building (including the altar) was still standing at this time. Nevertheless, the fact that these worshippers were dressed as mourners (note the reference to their beards being shaved, their clothes torn and their bodies gashed, v. 5), suggests that the destruction was significant and psychologically traumatic.

One of the first tasks of those who chose to return to Judah was to build an altar within the Temple complex so that they could re-establish regular sacrifices to the Lord. Then 'in the second year after their arrival' (Ezra 3.8) they started the reconstruction of the Temple proper. But when the foundations were laid, they were met with mixed emotions. Ezra 3.12–13 suggests that the older priests, Levites and heads of families who had seen the first Temple 'wept with a loud voice when they saw this house'. Clearly, the new Temple's foundations were not nearly as magnificent as those of the first, which had been constructed at the height of Solomon's empire.

It was not long before the rebuilding process began to encounter difficulties. The participation of some of the returnees appears to have been half-hearted at best, with priority given to their own needs and comfort rather than the Temple (cf. Hag. 1.4). Furthermore, local opposition from two groups – 'the adversaries of Judah and Benjamin' (who appear to have been those people settled in the former northern kingdom by the Assyrians, Ezra 4.1; cf. 2 Kings 17.24–28), and the 'people of the land' (which probably refers to the descendants of those Judahites who had not been taken into exile, Ezra 4.4) – appears to have succeeded in shutting down the rebuilding process, and the construction project languished for some time (Coogan, 2010: 420).

About 520 BC, work on the rebuilding of the Temple resumed in earnest. This was encouraged by **Haggai** and **Zechariah** who exhorted the people of God and their leaders (especially the governor Zerubbabel who is described in exalted terms, cf. Hag. 2.23; Zech. 4.14) to finish the job. Both prophets looked forward to a time of blessing and a dramatic worldwide act of God that would take place following the completion and consecration of the Temple. Financial support was received from both the Persian imperial coffers (Ezra 6.6–12) and wealthy exiles (Zech. 6.10–11) and, as a result, the reconstruction proceeded relatively swiftly. In 515 BC the rebuilt Temple, often referred to as the Second Temple, was dedicated, virtually 70 years after the first had been destroyed (cf. Jer. 25.11–12; 29.10).

Even though the Temple was rebuilt, the restored community in Jerusalem continued to experience difficulties and internal disputes into the fifth century BC. While the book of **Joel** is notoriously difficult to date, it may reflect conditions during this period. This book focuses on a number of threats to the nation, including a significant locust plague, loss of crops and military invasion, all of which are interpreted as anticipations of the imminent Day of the Lord. **Trito-Isaiah** (if its presence is accepted) and the book of **Malachi** address the internal problems and pressures plaguing the people. For Trito-Isaiah these include false worship, idolatry and the corruption of Israel's leaders, while Malachi highlights a widespread disregard for the covenant and cult, manifested in the tendency of some to offer sick animals and a failure to tithe (Mal. 1.6–8; 3.8). Such practices may have been a result of economic hardships (archaeological evidence indicates that most sites in Yehud remained relatively small and impoverished during this period), but a sense of disappointment, boredom (1.13) and religious scepticism (1.2; 2.17; 3.14–15) also seems to have played a role. Such sentiments may have resulted when the high hopes and expectations associated with Zerubbabel, the completion of the Temple, and the official restoration of the cult failed to be realized. Thus, the prophetic corpus comes to a close in much the same way as it opened with Amos – with a call to covenant faithfulness (Mal. 4.4) and a warning of the impending 'great and dreadful day of the LORD' (4.5–6 NIV).

Have you considered?
THE HISTORICAL CONTEXT OF JONAH AND DANIEL

Discussing the historical world of books such as Jonah and Daniel is complicated by the fact that their narrative context (i.e. the time in which the story is set) may not be the same as their historical context (i.e. the time in which the book was written).

Traditionally, the book of Jonah is located in the pre-exilic period. This is the date implied by the narrative itself (Jonah's destination, Nineveh, was an important Assyrian centre until the late seventh century BC) and is also suggested by the reference to a prophet named Jonah son of Amittai in 2 Kings 14.23–27. This prophet carried out his ministry during the time of King Jeroboam II (early to mid-eighth century BC), whose reign over the northern kingdom also witnessed the prophetic activity of Amos. Some scholars, however, suggest a later date of composition, locating the book in the post-exilic period. They point to indicators in the text (such as the reference to 'the king of Nineveh' in 3.6 which seems to reflect the view of a later author who was unaware that an Assyrian king would not have dwelt in Nineveh during the period) which they believe support their position.

The book of Daniel, on the other hand, is set in Babylon during the exilic period (mid-sixth century BC) and follows the travails of Daniel, a pious Jew, who rises to a position of prominence in the Babylonian administration but who remains faithful to the Lord. The book opens during the reign of Nebuchadnezzar (c.605–562 BC) and anticipates the fall of Babylon to the combined forces of the Medes and Persians in 539 BC (cf. 5.28). While evangelical scholars have usually (but not universally*) located the composition of the book shortly following Daniel's lifetime (late sixth to early fifth centuries BC), critical scholars have frequently suggested that the book was not completed until a later date, usually identified as the second century BC.[†] Adherents of this position point to chapter 11, which they argue contains references to the reign of Antiochus IV Epiphanes (175–164 BC), a significant persecutor of the Jews, as evidence for this hypothesis. They argue that the book was designed to encourage and console the Jews during this period of intense opposition.

---

* A dissenting voice, for example, is that of Goldingay, 1989.
[†] This is not to deny that much of the material, especially in chs 1—6, originated at an earlier stage.

2.5 Guidelines for analysing the historical world of the prophets

Due to their occasional nature, it is difficult to grasp the message of the prophetic books without having a clear understanding of the history of Israel and the broader geopolitical world in which the prophets lived. Three key events, in particular, form the backdrop for a large part of their message: the loss of the northern kingdom of Israel to the Assyrians in 722 BC, the loss of the southern kingdom of Judah to the Babylonians in 586 BC, and the return from exile under the Persians beginning in 538 BC. Much of the prophetic literature anticipates or provides a commentary on these pivotal, epoch-shifting developments.

So how does the exegete of the prophetic literature go about reconstructing its historical context?

2.5.1 Consult the biblical text

The first step involves reading the Bible, as the biblical text itself is often our primary source of contextual information.

As a starting point, it is worth reading through the prophetic book as a whole, preferably in one sitting, in order to gain a 'big picture' perspective of the times of the prophet, and the key issues he is addressing. Of course, this is easier to do for some books than others; a text such as Amos can be read in an hour or two whereas one of the major prophets, such as Jeremiah or Isaiah, might take considerably longer. In this case, it is worth consulting a secondary resource, such as a good Bible dictionary or the introduction to a commentary, which provides an introductory overview of the book as a whole. These resources are valuable even when working through one of the smaller prophetic books as their discussion should provide a helpful framework for your own reading of the text.

As you work through the prophetic book, try to reconstruct the situation into which the author is speaking. You may wish to take notes about the audience and the problems it is facing. As you are reading the text, an important question to keep in mind is: 'What was the spiritual state of the nation?' This involves considering the people's circumstances, their relationship with God, and any areas in which they were struggling.

Going deeper:
THE PROPHETIC AUTHOR

In addition to considering the situation of the audience, you may also wish to reflect on the prophet who is responsible for communicating God's word. This is especially important for those books where the prophet himself is, to a certain extent, the message (e.g. Jonah, Jeremiah, Hosea and Ezekiel). Familiarize yourself with the prophet's background, identity, position among God's people, and significant life experiences. All these factors will have shaped the prophet's message.

After you have worked through the prophetic book itself, it is worth considering any relevant material from elsewhere in the Bible. The very first verse of a prophetic book usually gives you some idea of its broad historical context (e.g. Amos 1.1 indicates that the prophet's ministry took place during the reigns of Uzziah of Judah and Jeroboam II of Israel, two years before the earthquake, c.760–755 BC) and this should allow you to identify what else you may need to read.[17] For the pre-exilic prophets, this will usually involve consulting the relevant section from the book of Kings and, time permitting, Chronicles, keeping in mind that the information contained in Chronicles is generally viewed as being less historically reliable than that found in Kings. For the prophets at work during the exilic period, the book of Lamentations may provide some insight into the situation in Judah following the Babylonian destruction of Jerusalem. For the post-exilic prophets, Ezra and Nehemiah may shed some light on the situation and issues they faced.

At this point, it is worth noting that the historical context of a prophetic book is not always clear. For example, Joel has been dated by different

---

[17] It should be acknowledged that the historical accuracy of these superscriptions is sometimes questioned as they are generally viewed as later, editorial insertions.

scholars to the pre-exilic, exilic and post-exilic periods. Obadiah is usually located shortly following the fall of Jerusalem in 586 BC, but a date in the post-exilic period (c. late sixth to early fifth century) is not out of the question. In these cases the exegete needs to be cautious in his or her use of external historical information (i.e. historical information that is not found within the book itself) to interpret the biblical text. Fortunately, even those texts that provide no concrete indications of their date or authorship will usually contain enough information for you to identify the kind of circumstances the prophet is addressing and the aims the prophet had in relation to these (Goldingay, 1995: 173). For example, Joel (or at least the first two chapters) needs to be understood against the background of a great locust plague, while Obadiah was produced at a time of significant hostility between Judah and Edom.

Once you have developed an awareness of the broad historical context of the book as a whole, you need to focus on the specific passage at hand. Read through the passage carefully, noting any historical-cultural features or details such as geographical references, political considerations, religious beliefs, allusions to historical events, economic practices, dynamics of family life, social customs, etc. Make sure you understand the significance of these. This may require you to consult secondary sources.

2.5.2 Consult secondary sources

Going deeper:
WHAT ABOUT EXTRABIBLICAL PRIMARY SOURCES?

Texts from the ancient Near East may shed light on the historical world of the prophets by giving us an insight into the broader international context of the prophets' message and illuminating religious beliefs and practices alluded to in the biblical text (e.g. the worship of Baal in ancient Israel). Generally speaking, the relevant documents are discussed in good secondary sources, especially commentaries. If you wish to examine them for yourself, there are a number of recent volumes which present these documents in an accessible format. Good options include Arnold and Beyer, 2002 and Hallo, 2003.

Reconstructing the historical world of the prophets is not something you can or should attempt to do entirely on your own. Good historical reconstruction is a difficult process, and requires a significant, current knowledge of a range of disciplines (including biblical studies, ancient Near Eastern studies, archaeology, etc.) which the beginning exegete is unlikely to possess. This is one area, therefore, where secondary sources are particularly valuable and need to be consulted. Fortunately, there is a wealth of such resources available, written with the needs of virtually every student of the Bible in mind.

You will find four types of resources particularly valuable:

1 *Bible dictionaries.* These should contain relevant articles on the book as a whole as well as entries on the key historical-cultural details which are found in the text.
2 *Bible commentaries.* More detailed volumes will include both an introductory section (which usually provides a good overview of the background of the book) and a verse-by-verse or section-by-section analysis of the text itself.
3 *Introductions to the Old Testament.* These will usually provide basic background details about the individual books as well as an overview of their message.
4 *Other resources.* There is a plethora of additional resources to help you analyse the historical world of the prophets. Two types of books will be particularly valuable: those which focus on everyday life in ancient Israel and archaeological handbooks which summarize the key archaeological data in a format that is suitable for the non-specialist.

Suggested examples of some of these resources are listed in the 'Further reading' section below.

2.6 Potential problems to avoid

There are three main pitfalls that we should seek to avoid when reconstructing the historical world of the prophets.

2.6.1 Substituting historical research for exegesis

The ultimate goal of historical research when done in the context of exegesis is to help shed light on the meaning of the biblical text. It is possible, however, to get so caught up in studying the historical background of the passage that we lose sight of the text itself. If this is the case, we have substituted the means (historical research) for the end (a better understanding of the passage). If your historical research is not helping you achieve a better understanding of the text, then you should look to reduce the amount of time and space you are devoting to it.

The key to avoiding this problem is being able to identify exactly what are the important facts and issues related to your passage (and the book of which it is a part) that will help you better understand it. A helpful question to consider when you are wading through the wealth of information relating to a text's historical context is: 'Of everything I could learn and say about these contexts, what are the key facts and issues related to this passage that will affect my interpretation of it?' (Gorman, 2001: 72).

2.6.2 Overgeneralizing

Cultures are incredibly complex phenomena. They embody and are shaped by a variety of social, economic, political and religious factors, to name a few.

While we may be aware of the various influences and dynamics that are at play in our own native culture, it is more difficult to see the depth of complexities that are present in others, especially those which are separated from us by a vast historical and social gap. As a result, we will tend to over-simplify realities and fail to recognize the presence of diversity. One example of such oversimplification and overgeneralization would be to assume that all ancient Israelites thought or believed the same thing on a given issue. This is unlikely to have been the case. Just as the modern world is marked by a plurality of views and opinions, so too was the ancient.[18]

In order to overcome this potential problem, we must be careful of the statements we make and ensure we have worked through the available resources closely. Quality secondary sources should open our eyes to the complexities of life and belief in ancient Israel.

2.6.3 Mirror reading

Discerning the situation of the prophet's audience can be a tricky business. One potential problem is 'mirror reading'. This practice assumes that *every* exhortation or argument in a text reflects a problem being experienced by the text's audience. While this may often be the case, we should not automatically assume it to be so.

Since we need to use clues from the prophetic book itself in our historical reconstructions, mirror reading is all too easy to do. To overcome this problem, we need to make sure that we are drawing upon the widest possible range of evidence, including other relevant sections from the biblical text, pertinent ancient Near Eastern sources, and the findings of archaeology. These may help to provide a fuller picture and/or balance out the prophet's often polemical portrayal of his audience's situation.

2.7 Summary

The occasional nature of the prophetic literature requires us to pay attention to its historical context when doing our interpretive work. 'It is striking that the scriptural material that most overtly claims a divine origin is also the material that most consistently draws attention to its own historical background and thus to the need to understand it against that background' (Goldingay, 1995: 167). Such historical work, which requires serious engagement with both the biblical text and secondary sources, is well worth the effort as it has the potential to provide us with a richer, fuller and more accurate understanding of the message of Israel's prophets.

---

[18] For example, the Old Testament suggests that there was a multiplicity of views within ancient Israel even on such a fundamental issue as which god or gods the people should worship.

Further reading

History of prophecy

Blenkinsopp, J. *A History of Prophecy in Israel*, revised and enlarged. Louisville: WJKP, 1996.

History of ancient Israel

Critical: Coogan, M. (ed.). *The Oxford History of the Biblical World*. Oxford: Oxford University Press, 1998.

Evangelical: Provan, I., V. P. Long and T. Longman III. *A Biblical History of Israel*. Louisville: WJKP, 2003.

Ancient Near Eastern context

Sassoon, J. (ed.). *Civilizations of the Ancient Near East*, vols 1–4. Peabody: Hendrickson, 2000.

Walton, J. *Ancient Near Eastern Thought and the Old Testament: Introducing the Conceptual World of the Hebrew Bible*. Grand Rapids: Baker, 2006.

Bible dictionary

Multi-volume: Freedman, D. (ed.). *The Anchor Bible Dictionary*, vols 1–6. New York: Doubleday, 1992.

Single volume: Powell, M. (gen. ed.). *HarperCollins Bible Dictionary*, revised and updated. New York: HarperOne, 2011.

Introduction to the Old Testament

Critical: Coogan, M. *The Old Testament: A Historical and Literary Introduction to the Hebrew Scriptures*, 2nd edn. Oxford: Oxford University Press, 2010.

Evangelical: LaSor, W., D. Hubbard and F. Bush. *Old Testament Survey: The Message, Form, and Background of the Old Testament*, 2nd edn. Grand Rapids: Eerdmans, 1996.

Other books

Borowski, O. *Daily Life in Biblical Times*, SBLABS 5. Atlanta: SBL, 2003.

King, P. and L. Stager. *Life in Biblical Israel*, LAI. Louisville: WJKP, 2001.

Mazar, A. *Archaeology of the Land of the Bible, vol. 1: 10,000–586 B.C.E.*, ABRL. New York: Doubleday, 1992.

Stern, E. *Archaeology of the Land of the Bible, vol. 2: 732–332 B.C.E.*, ABRL. New York: Doubleday, 2001.

3

The theological world of the prophets

3.1 Introduction

As we have seen in Chapter 2, part of the reason it is difficult to interpret the Old Testament prophets stems from the fact that they come from a different historical and social world from our own. A second complicating factor is that they operate within a distinct conceptual and ideological framework or worldview, a framework which is, in large parts, foreign to many modern readers of the Bible. The second world we need to consider when interpreting the prophets, therefore, is their theological world.

Essentially, the theological world of the prophets includes the beliefs, ideologies and assumptions, especially regarding God, the Israelite people and the Israelite king, which shaped their message. Contrary to some popular belief, the prophets were not creative and inventive geniuses who wove their messages out of thin air. Their works may contain unique elements and emphases, but for the most part they were engaging with and responding to (sometimes positively, sometimes negatively) common and widespread pre-existing ideas. For example, Amos' stern warning regarding the Day of the Lord (Amos 5.18–20) gains its power, not because he is inventing the concept outright, but because he appears to be subverting the pre-existing expectations of at least some of his contemporaries.

Most introductory textbooks to the prophets usually contain discrete discussions of the theology of each prophetic book (for some good examples, see the 'Further reading' section below). There is value in this approach; it allows us to hear the unique voice of each individual within the larger prophetic choir. In this chapter, however, my goal is different – I want to lay out and explain the basic theological framework which most of the prophets operated within as a means of establishing a conceptual context for understanding their writings. This is essential information which the prophets assumed their audience would be familiar with and which we need to understand if we hope to grasp more fully their message.

In order to explain the prophets' theological framework, I have chosen to focus on two key traditions which were particularly influential in shaping not just the prophets but the Old Testament writings as a whole. In Old Testament studies, a tradition is defined as 'a complex of beliefs associated with particular persons, events, places, institutions, symbols, or rituals' (Broyles, 2001a: 44). The Old Testament contains numerous traditions, including Creation, ancestors, exodus, theophany, conquest and Yahweh war. The two traditions which are particularly important for interpreting the prophets are: (i) Sinai and the establishment of a covenant between the Lord and the Israelite people, and (ii) Zion and the establishment of a covenant between the Lord and David (and his descendants). As will be seen in the discussion below, these traditions lie just below the surface of many prophetic texts.

Going deeper:
CONCEPTUALIZING OLD TESTAMENT TRADITIONS

Perhaps the best way of grasping the significance of traditions for the prophets is to consider the New Testament's use of the Old Testament. When composing their work, the New Testament authors were able to draw from a large body of pre-existing written texts to support and develop their arguments. These shaped their work both implicitly (i.e. such texts helped to form their worldview) and explicitly (e.g. through the use of quotation). In a similar fashion, the works of the Old Testament authors, including the prophets, have been shaped, both directly and indirectly, by a large body of pre-existing, largely oral traditions.*

---

* Some Old Testament authors draw on pre-existing (but no longer extant) written documents. For example, Joshua 10.13 quotes from the 'Book of Jashar'. Such citations, however, are largely restricted to narrative texts; there is no clear evidence that the authors of the prophetic texts used such pre-existing works.

In the second part of this chapter, I will focus on the exegetical implications of the fact that the prophets frequently employ and transform pre-existing traditions. In particular, we will look at analysing theologically 'loaded' words and phrases, utilizing a modified form of analysis known as tradition criticism, which seeks to discern what an author presumes, intends and insinuates through the use of traditional language.

3.2 Sinai and the Lord's covenant with the Israelite people[1]

To understand much of the prophetic message we need to journey back to the origins of the nation as narrated in the book of Exodus. Following their deliverance from slavery in Egypt, the Hebrew people wandered in the wilderness for a period of approximately three months before arriving at Mt Sinai. There they entered into a covenant with the Lord.

---

[1] This covenant is sometimes referred to as the 'Mosaic Covenant'; however, I find this terminology unhelpful as the primary participant here is the people as a whole, not Moses the individual (unlike in the Abrahamic and Davidic Covenants).

The Sinai Covenant resembles 'suzerain–vassal' treaties which were relatively widespread in the ancient Near East. These treaties were established between a powerful sovereign (the suzerain) and a weaker king or ruler (the vassal), and were designed to regulate the relationship between the two kingdoms. They usually consisted of three key elements:[2]

1 *A historical prologue* which describes the suzerain's actions on behalf of the vassal that form the basis for the treaty;
2 *A list of stipulations* which records the expectations the suzerain places on the vassal – the primary expectation is usually complete and absolute loyalty to the suzerain;
3 *A list of blessings and curses* which lays out the consequences of the vassal adhering to, or failing to adhere to, the previously mentioned stipulations: continued loyalty will bring blessings, disobedience a series of horrific curses. The inclusion of the latter, in particular, is designed to 'encourage' the vassal's obedience to the stipulations of the treaty.

Going deeper:
EXAMPLES OF VASSAL TREATIES FROM THE ANCIENT NEAR EAST

Numerous examples of suzerain–vassal treaties have been found from the ancient Near East, including Hittite versions dated to the mid-second millennium BC and Neo-Assyrian exemplars (sometimes referred to as 'Loyalty Oaths') from around the seventh century BC.

> The Assyrian documents tend to give many curses, while the Hittite treaties offer more detailed blessings. Typical stipulations include loyalty, payment of tribute, reception of ambassadors, provision for garrison troops, participation in military campaigns when requested, information concerning conspiracies, and extradition of enemies.
>
> (Walton, 2006: 69)

Translations of these documents can be found in *COS*, vol. 2: 91–105, 329–32 and *ANET*, 199–205, 529–34.

These elements are all present within the context of the Sinai Covenant, where Yahweh is portrayed as the gracious suzerain and Israel the (dis)obedient vassal. Exodus 19 is a key text. Following the arrival of the people in the Sinai wilderness, Moses goes up the mountain where he is addressed by the Lord. The Lord begins by declaring his gracious work on Israel's behalf: 'Thus

---

[2] Scholars usually identify five or six key features of ancient Near Eastern suzerain–vassal treaties: preamble (introducing the parties to the covenant), historical prologue (rehearsing the parties' past relationship), stipulations, requirements for the preservation of the treaty document, divine witnesses, and blessings and curses. For further details see Mendenhall and Herion, 1992: 1180–3. In my discussion I have chosen to focus on those elements which are particularly relevant for interpreting the prophets.

you shall say to the house of Jacob, and tell the Israelites: You have seen what I did to the Egyptians, and how I bore you on eagles' wings and brought you to myself' (vv. 3–4). This section functions as the *historical prologue* to the covenant – it contains a brief, succinct description of the Lord's liberation of Israel from its Egyptian oppressors and his role in bringing them through the wilderness. The Lord then goes on to explain the privileged status the people will have as a result of the covenant: 'Now therefore, if you obey my voice and keep my covenant, you shall be my treasured possession out of all the peoples. Indeed, the whole earth is mine, but you shall be for me a priestly kingdom and a holy nation' (vv. 5–6). After Moses has repeated the Lord's words to the elders, the people as one agree to the Lord's demands: 'Everything that the LORD has spoken we will do' (v. 8).

> **Going deeper:**
> **ISRAEL AS THE LORD'S 'TREASURED POSSESSION' (EXOD. 19.5)**
>
> The Hebrew word translated 'treasured possession' is *s^{e}gullâ*. This word refers to an individual's, often the king's, personal property or wealth. In 1 Chronicles 29.3 David announces, 'in addition to all that I have provided for the holy house, I have a treasure of my own (*s^{e}gullâ*) of gold and silver, and because of my devotion to the house of my God I give it to the house of my God'. By using this noun with reference to Israel, the Lord is declaring that the nation is uniquely valued and owned by the Lord, to use as he wills. Interestingly, the cognate term is used in an Ugaritic text with reference to the vassal of a Hittite king (Lipiński, 1999: 146).

The *stipulations* of the covenant between the Lord and Israel are then laid out, beginning in Exodus 20 and running through to Leviticus 25.[3] These are repeated in Deuteronomy where they are applied to the situation of the Israelite people who are about to enter the promised land. Central to these is the Ten Commandments (or Decalogue) which is recorded in Exodus 20 and Deuteronomy 5. As suggested above, ancient Near Eastern suzerain–vassal treaties laid one fundamental expectation or obligation on the vassal: the vassal was expected to be completely loyal to the suzerain and not defect to another power. Thus, the key stipulations for the Sinai Covenant, the Ten Commandments, begin with the declaration that Israel is to have no other gods before the Lord, and is not to worship idols (Exod.

---

[3] This is a large block of material and it is possible to subdivide the stipulations into smaller sections. It is common, for example, to view Exodus 20—23 as a unity, sometimes referred to as 'the Book of the Covenant' (cf. Exod. 24.7) or 'the Covenant Code', which culminates in a covenant ratification ceremony involving sacrifices in Exodus 24.

20.2–6; cf. Deut. 5.6–10). The second half of the Ten Commandments focuses on interpersonal relationships, revealing another key emphasis of the Sinai stipulations: Israel was to be a community whose life was regulated by justice.

Going deeper:
THE TWO VERSIONS OF THE TEN COMMANDMENTS

Exodus 20 and Deuteronomy 5 offer two slightly different versions of the Ten Commandments. For example, in the Exodus version the theological basis for Sabbath observance is God's rest following the six days of creation (20.8–11). In Deuteronomy 5.12–15, on the other hand, the command is premised on Israel's experience of deliverance from their slavery in Egypt. In both cases, however, the Ten Commandments are the first laws that are recorded within a larger block of regulations (Deuteronomy 5 begins a section which runs through to chapter 11), suggesting their central, fundamental and foundational importance to all of Israel's law.

The consequences for covenant obedience and disobedience, the *list of blessings and curses*, are hinted at in various passages in the book of Exodus (e.g. 22.24; 23.21, 33) and developed more fully in Leviticus 26 (cf. the similar list in Deut. 28). These are intended to 'encourage' the vassal's adherence to the stipulations of the treaty. The blessings for covenant obedience and faithfulness are laid out first. These focus on the material well-being of the people and include agricultural abundance (vv. 4–5), peace and victory in battle (vv. 6–8), numerous offspring (v. 9) and the Lord's abiding presence (vv. 11–12). The covenant curses, which would be instituted should the people fail to obey the stipulations of the covenant and prove themselves to be disloyal to Yahweh, are listed second. There are more of these (this follows common ancient Near Eastern practice) and they tend to be quite graphic. They include disease (v. 16), defeat (vv. 17, 25), lack of agricultural produce (v. 20), plague and pestilence (vv. 21, 25), attack by wild animals (v. 22), destruction (vv. 30–31), deportation from the land (v. 33) and utter desolation (vv. 32–33). It should be recognized, however, that divine cursing is not the final or ultimate word in Leviticus 26. The Lord promises that

> if they confess their iniquity and the iniquity of their ancestors ... I will not spurn them, or abhor them so as to destroy them utterly and break my covenant with them; for I am the LORD their God; but I will remember in their favour the covenant with their ancestors whom I brought out of the land of Egypt in the sight of the nations, to be their God: I am the LORD.   (vv. 40, 44–45)

Should the people humble themselves and make amends for their iniquity (v. 41), the possibility of a favourable divine response remains.

Going deeper:
WHY ARE THERE SO FEW REFERENCES TO THE SINAI COVENANT IN THE WRITINGS OF THE EARLY PROPHETS?

Explicit references to the Sinai Covenant are not common in the prophetic books, especially the earlier ones. For example, the 12 minor prophets contain a total of nine references, with only two of these (Hos. 6.7; 8.1) possibly coming from the pre-exilic period (Rata, 2012: 99). Various proposals have been put forward to explain the absence of covenantal terminology. For example, critical scholars, such as Perlitt, Nicholson and McKenzie, have proposed an essentially historical explanation, claiming that the lack of references may be due to the fact that the concept of a divine–human covenant itself only 'came to full expression relatively late in Israel's history' (McKenzie, 2000: 25). Lindblom has developed a more theologically focused hypothesis:

> The relative paucity of references to the covenant in the pre-exilic prophets is presumably to be ascribed to the fact that the juridical character of this idea led the people to make claims on their God as of right and to cherish ambitious dreams of supposedly inevitable glorious future. It was a prime task of the pre-exilic prophets to combat such false illusions. (1963: 329)

It should be recognized, however, that even though explicit covenantal terminology may be rare, the presence of covenant motifs and realities in the prophetic writings is more common and widespread – the oracles of the prophets embody a 'matrix of [covenantal] ideas' (Mendenhall and Herion, 1992: 1190). For further discussion of the link between the prophets and the Sinai Covenant, see Rata, 2012; Robertson, 2004 (especially ch. 6).

The importance of the Sinai Covenant traditions for the prophets is easy to see. The prophets are not essentially radicals or innovators; instead, they are better characterized as traditionalists and conservatives who are responsible for calling Israel back to their covenantal obligations to the Lord. In fact, Fee and Stuart (2003: 184) refer to the prophets as 'covenant enforcement mediators', highlighting the fact that the demands they make and the judgements they announce closely follow the stipulations and curses of the Sinai Covenant. Although explicit covenantal language may not be common (especially in the earlier prophetic books), all the prophets assume a close relationship between the nation and the Lord which involves loyalty and specific religious and social expectations.[4] Furthermore, the charges or indictments which the prophets bring against the people often reflect a failure to adhere to the key stipulations of the Sinai Covenant. Idolatry in all its manifestations is frequently condemned

---

[4] This close relationship is seen, for example, in Jeremiah's repeated use of the so-called covenant formula, 'I will be your God, and you shall be my people' (Exod. 6.7; Lev. 26.12; cf. Jer. 7.23; 11.4; 30.22).

Figure 3.1 Judahite female clay 'pillar figurines' from Jerusalem, Beer-Sheba, Tel Erani (eighth to sixth century BC). The precise function of these figurines remains unknown; however, some scholars have suggested that they may have served as idols

© Damien Rey / Wikimedia Commons. CC By-SA-3.0.

(see Fig. 3.1), with Hays declaring, 'The prophets preach continuously against idolatry. It is a central feature of most prophetic books and is usually introduced early in each prophetic book' (2010: 65).[5] The same is true for the prophets' critique of social injustice (e.g. Isa. 1; Jer. 5.20–29; Amos 5), the presence of which reflects a lack of care and concern for one's fellow Israelites, and thus a serious breakdown within the covenanted community. The close relationship between the prophets' accusations and the Sinai stipulations is perhaps seen most clearly in Hosea's allegations against the inhabitants of the northern kingdom, which mirror the second half of the Ten Commandments: 'Swearing, lying, and murder, and stealing and adultery break out; bloodshed follows bloodshed' (Hos. 4.2). Thus, the prophets appear to operate within a covenant-shaped worldview, even if they do not directly utilize explicit covenantal terminology as much as we might expect.

Sinai covenant traditions were also influential in shaping the prophets' hope and future expectations regarding the Lord's work of salvation and restoration for his people following exile. Jeremiah, for example, speaks of a 'new covenant' which will involve the Lord putting his law within the people and writing it on their hearts (Jer. 31.33). Although Jeremiah seeks to distinguish this covenant from the one enacted at Sinai ('It will not be like the covenant that I made with their ancestors when I took them by the hand to bring them out of the land of Egypt – a covenant that they broke, though

---

[5] Prophetic texts that condemn idolatry include Isa. 2.8–9, 18–20; Jer. 2.20–28; 10.1–16; Ezek. 6.9–13; 8.1–18; Hos. 4.10–19; 8.4–5; 10.5–6; 11.2; Amos 5.26; 7.9; Mic. 1.5–7; Hab. 2.18–20; Zeph. 1.4–6; Zech. 13.2.

I was their husband', 31.32), it is clear nonetheless that there is significant continuity between the two (both, for example, contain law and both serve to secure the same objective – 'I will be their God, and they shall be my people'), and that the expectations associated with the new covenant are best understood in the light of Sinai traditions.[6] Furthermore, prophetic proclamations of anticipated agricultural abundance and prosperity seem to link back with the blessings for covenant faithfulness. This is seen, for example, when one compares Amos 9.13 ('The time is surely coming, says the LORD, when the one who ploughs shall overtake the one who reaps, and the treader of grapes the one who sows the seed; the mountains shall drip sweet wine, and all the hills shall flow with it') with Leviticus 26.5 ('Your threshing shall overtake the vintage, and the vintage shall overtake the sowing; you shall eat your bread to the full, and live securely in your land'). A similar dynamic (i.e. the use of covenantal blessings to describe the future salvific work of God) seems to be at play when one considers promises connected with peace and safety in the land.

Have you considered?
THE THEOLOGICAL FRAMEWORK OF THE 'ORACLES AGAINST THE NATIONS'

While the Sinai traditions provide a helpful framework for understanding much of the prophetic writings, they are perhaps less relevant for explaining those sections commonly referred to as 'oracles against the nations' such as we find in Isaiah (13.1—21.17; 23.1–18; 34.1–15), Jeremiah (46.1—51.64), Ezekiel (25.1—32.32), Amos (1.3—2.3), Obadiah and Nahum. In these passages the Lord graphically announces his intention to judge the surrounding nations, including Egypt, Assyria, Babylonia and Edom. Here the basis for the Lord's judgement is not the stipulations of the Sinai Covenant (after all, these nations were not even present at Sinai); other themes, such as war crimes or acts of inhumanity, wickedness, arrogance and pride, are key. A number of nations are also indicted for the way they have treated the people of God. The theological framework for these oracles is twofold:

1 Yahweh is Lord of all nations (not just Israel), and expects all people to act according to certain standards (interpersonally and internationally). Failure to do so will result in divine judgement.
2 Yahweh is Lord of Israel and will attack those who oppress his people.

---

[6] Although other prophets do not use the title 'new covenant', similar expectations seem to be present in other books, including Isaiah, Ezekiel, Hosea and Malachi. Ezekiel, for example, speaks of a future 'covenant of peace' (Ezek. 34.25; 37.26). For a fuller discussion of these passages see Williamson, 2007: 146–81.

Figure 3.2 Restored stepped stone structure/wall built in the Iron
Age (possibly Jebusite), Jerusalem

© Deror Avi / Wikimedia Commons.

3.3 Zion and the Lord's covenant with David

Going deeper:
A BRIEF HISTORY OF JERUSALEM UP TO THE REIGN OF DAVID

A basic understanding of the history of Jerusalem is helpful for grasping the
nature of the Zion traditions. Jerusalem was probably first settled some time during
the middle to late fourth millennium BC, as pottery dating from the Chaolithic
period (c.3500 BC) has been discovered on the Ophel, above the Gihon Spring
(King, 1992: 752). Archaeological and textual remains suggest that the city was
continuously occupied: it is mentioned in Egyptian execration texts from the nineteenth to eighteenth centuries BC and again in the Amarna letters dated to the
fourteenth century BC. By the time of the emergence of Israel in the land of Canaan
(c. twelfth to eleventh century BC), the city was settled by the Jebusites, being a
well-defended Jebusite stronghold (see Fig. 3.2). Although Judges 1.8 suggests
that the tribe of Judah captured Jerusalem as part of the conquest of the promised
land, Jerusalem did not definitively fall into Israelite hands until it was seized by
David and his band of mercenaries some time around the beginning of the tenth
century BC (2 Sam. 5.6–7).

David was a smart politician and quickly established Jerusalem as the political,
religious and administrative capital of his kingdom. The reason for the choice of

Jerusalem was probably twofold: (i) it was centrally located between the northern and southern tribes, and (ii) it was 'extraterritorial' in that it had not previously been part of a tribal inheritance. (While Jerusalem was technically within the territory allocated to Benjamin, it had never been occupied by the Benjaminites.) In order to establish the city as the religious hub for his kingdom, one of David's first acts as king was to bring the most important Israelite religious item – the ark of the covenant, the symbol of divine presence – from Shiloh to Jerusalem.

The second tradition complex we need to consider when interpreting the prophets involves the Lord, David and Zion. The term 'Zion' is used more than 90 times in the prophetic books and usually refers either to the city of Jerusalem or a specific section of the city, the hill on which the Temple stood.[7] 'Zion traditions' or 'Zion theology' characteristically denote a cluster of beliefs surrounding the divine King, Yahweh, the human king, David (and his successors), and the royal residence (Jerusalem and/or the Temple). This complex set of interrelated religious and political beliefs played an important role in justifying and legitimating the Davidic monarchy, and forms the conceptual background to a number of prophetic texts, particularly from the book of Isaiah.[8] In fact, according to Sawyer:

> The Zion traditions, including beliefs about the Davidic royal family, constitute the most highly developed and influential theme in biblical prophecy. Even for prophets like Hosea, Amos, and Ezekiel who may never have uttered a word in Jerusalem itself, the city and its Davidic dynasty play an important role.
>
> (1993: 56)

3.3.1 The Lord as King

The fundamental basis for Zion theology is the belief that Israel's God, Yahweh, is the divine King who rules over heaven and earth. He is the Great King (Pss. 47.2; 95.3) who rules over all people, all nations and all the heavenly beings. Psalm 47.7–9 provides concrete expression of this belief:

> For God is the king of all the earth;
>   sing praises with a psalm.
> God is king over the nations;
>   God sits on his holy throne.
> The princes of the peoples gather
>   as the people of the God of Abraham.
> For the shields of the earth belong to God;
>   he is highly exalted.

---

[7] 'Zion' is also used in the Old Testament to refer to the pre-Israelite, Jebusite fortress in Jerusalem and the people of Israel. For further discussion of the various ways in which the term could be used, see Otto, 2003: 333–65; Strong, 1997: 1314–21.

[8] For further discussion of the ideological function of the Zion traditions, see Gravett et al., 2008: 324–36.

Ancient Near Eastern parallels:
DIVINE KINGSHIP AND THE DEFEAT OF THE FORCES OF CHAOS

Canaanite and Mesopotamian literature also connects the elevation of a particular god as king within their respective pantheons to the defeat of chaotic forces (see Fig. 3.3). This is seen most clearly in the Akkadian document *Enuma Eliš*, where Marduk's rise to head of the pantheon of the gods is linked with his defeat of the rebel Tiamat, a chaos monster and primordial goddess of the ocean. The conflict between the great divine king and chaos thus appears to have been a common way ancient Near Eastern people formed their theology: 'Israel . . . expressed its beliefs about the Lord in similar terms, while at the same time affirming the superiority and uniqueness of Yahweh' (Strong, 1997: 1315).

Figure 3.3 Depiction of the Hittite sky god killing the serpent-dragon Illuyankas (850–800 BC)

© Tayfun Bilgin / Wikimedia Commons.

Yahweh's kingship is assumed in the Sinai traditions; his position as suzerain is a given. (In other words, there is no real description of how Yahweh became King.) In Zion theology, however, the Lord's kingship is explained – the basis for Yahweh's rule is his defeat of the forces of chaos, a common motif in ancient Near Eastern literature. There are a number of allusions to this event in the book of Psalms,[9] with Psalm 74.12–14 the most explicit:

> Yet God my King is from of old,
>   working salvation in the earth.
> You divided the sea by your might;
>   you broke the heads of the dragons in the waters.
> You crushed the heads of Leviathan;
>   you gave him as food for the creatures of the wilderness.

---

[9] See also Pss. 89.9–13; 93; 104.1–9.

Figure 3.4 Chipiez's reconstruction of the interior of the Solomonic Temple

Singer, I. (ed.). *The Jewish Encyclopedia*, vol. 12. New York: Funk and Wagnalls, 1912, p. 93.

Note here the link between the Lord's kingship and his defeat of the 'sea', 'dragons' and 'Leviathan', all of which were sources or forces of chaos in the ancient world.[10]

3.3.2 Zion as the Lord's residence

A second key feature of Zion theology is the belief that the Great King Yahweh has chosen Zion as his earthly dwelling place and imperial capital (Roberts, 2009: 987).

Following the death of David, Solomon launched a number of important building projects, including the royal palace and adjoining Temple (see Fig. 3.4). The construction of the latter consolidated Jerusalem as the religious centre of the kingdom and confirmed Zion/Jerusalem not only as the abode of the Davidic dynasty but also as the city of God. In fact, the biblical authors speak of Yahweh selecting Zion to be his earthly home; it was the place where he had chosen to 'put his name'. Thus Psalm 132.13–14 declares:

> For the LORD has chosen Zion;
>   he has desired it for his habitation:
> 'This is my resting-place for ever;
>   here I will reside, for I have desired it.'

Likewise, in Psalm 78.67–69 the psalmist announces:

> He rejected the tent of Joseph,
>   he did not choose the tribe of Ephraim;
> but he chose the tribe of Judah,
>   Mount Zion, which he loves.
> He built his sanctuary like the high heavens,
>   like the earth, which he has founded for ever.[11]

Because the Lord has chosen Zion as his earthly dwelling place it is described in the Old Testament in glorious, cosmic terms as befitting its King. For example, Psalm 48.2 depicts the Lord's holy mountain as 'beautiful in elevation', 'the joy of all the earth', and 'the heights (or peak) of Zaphon' (my translation).[12] On a purely literal level, these statements are false:

1 Zion is only relatively modest in height (approx. 725 metres), and is not even the tallest mountain in the immediate vicinity (the nearby Mount of Olives, for example, is higher at approx. 770 metres);
2 Jerusalem was the capital of a kingdom which remained relatively insignificant throughout its history, at least from an international perspective;
3 'Zaphon' was the name of a mountain located far to the north of Jerusalem, the sacred mountain of Baal in Canaanite mythology and the place where the assembly of the gods met (cf. Isa. 14.13).

---

[10] For further discussion of this myth and its presence in the Old Testament, see Mobley, 2012.

[11] See also Pss. 2.6; 68.15–16.

[12] In the NRSV the phrase I have rendered 'the heights (or peak) of Zaphon' is translated 'in the far north'. This is due to the fact that the underlying Hebrew word (*ṣāpōn*) can mean either Zaphon (a mountain to the north of Israel) or the direction north. For further details, see Lipiński, 2003: 435–43.

Why, then, has the psalmist decided to describe Zion in this fashion? This is due to the fact that the author is expressing an ideological understanding of Zion, rather than a strictly topographical or geographical one. These descriptors emphasize that Zion is the cosmic locus of God's presence, rule and authority. By identifying Zion with Zaphon (Ps. 48.2) and El's palace (Ps. 46.4), the author is asserting that Zion is the true dwelling place of God. This is no mere mountain – it is the threshold between heaven and earth.

Going deeper:
THE RIVER OF PARADISE WHICH FLOWS FROM ZION

Another significant element in the ideological portrayal of Zion is the presence of a river 'whose streams make glad the city of God, the holy habitation of the Most High' (Ps. 46.4). In reality, the closest thing to a river in Jerusalem is the modest water channel fed by the Gihon Spring. It has been suggested that the background for this somewhat exaggerated description is the location of the great god El's abode 'at the source of the rivers, amidst the springs of the two deeps' (*KTU* 1.2 iii 4). If this is the case, the use of the riverine motif in Psalm 46 reinforces Zion as the true dwelling place of God.

It is also worth noting that the name 'Gihon' is used with reference to one of the branches of the river which flows out of the primordial garden of Eden to water and fertilize the whole world (Gen. 2.10–13) (see Fig. 3.5). We encounter a confluence of these elements (Zion, a river and prosperity/fertility) in Ezekiel 47 where a great river flows out of Zion's Temple, bringing with it fertility and life even for the 'Dead' Sea.

The fact that God had taken up residence on Mt Zion has a number of important theological and practical implications. It means, for example, that Zion is depicted as the place from which God speaks and acts. The prophet Amos declares:

> The LORD roars from Zion,
> and utters his voice from Jerusalem;
> the pastures of the shepherds wither,
> and the top of Carmel dries up.   (Amos 1.2)

As the point of contact between the divine and human realms, it makes sense for the prophet to describe God's activity as emanating from this location.

Furthermore, because the Lord has chosen Zion, he will protect the city. Even though the forces of chaos and Israel's earthly enemies may assail the city, they will not be victorious. The Lord's presence means that the city, and its inhabitants, are safe. Thus, in Psalm 46 the psalmist declares:

Figure 3.5 A wall painting depicting the investiture of Zimri-
Lim, from Mari (eighteenth century BC). The goddess Ištar,
who is standing on a lion, presents Zimri-Lim with symbols
of authority. Note also the rivers of water and the paradisiacal
garden setting

© Marie-Lan Nguyen / Wikimedia Commons.

> God is our refuge and strength,
> a very present help in trouble.
> Therefore we will not fear, though the earth should change,
> though the mountains shake in the heart of the sea;
> though its waters roar and foam,
> though the mountains tremble with its tumult. *Selah*
>
> There is a river whose streams make glad the city of God,
> the holy habitation of the Most High.
> God is in the midst of the city; it shall not be moved;
> God will help it when the morning dawns.
> The nations are in an uproar, the kingdoms totter;
> he utters his voice, the earth melts.
> The LORD of hosts is with us;
> the God of Jacob is our refuge. *Selah*
>
> (Ps. 46.1–7; cf. Ps. 48.1–5)

Beliefs regarding God's protection of Zion were probably reinforced by the
events of 701 BC. In that year the Assyrian king, Sennacherib, invaded Judah,
capturing all of the important cities apart from Jerusalem (for further details,
see Chapter 2). The dramatic survival of Jerusalem in the face of seemingly
overwhelming odds appears to have strengthened the conviction that the
Lord had indeed chosen and taken up residence in Zion and therefore the city
was inviolable.

Going deeper:
THE PROPHETS AND THE INVIOLABILITY OF JERUSALEM

Old Testament scholars have debated whether or not Israel understood the Lord's protection of Zion to be conditional. Some (e.g. Rohland and Day) have argued that the Lord's residence in Zion was the key factor in the city's inviolability, and thus the behaviour of the people was unimportant. Others (e.g. Clements) have suggested that this perspective was only a later, post-701 BC development and that originally there was no conception of an automatic guarantee of protection simply based on the Lord's presence.

The prophets themselves seem to view the Lord's protection as conditional. They downplay the notion that Zion was inviolable and emphasize that Yahweh, as the divine Lord of the city, expected piety and obedience from its inhabitants. For example, while continuing to emphasize the importance of the Temple itself, Isaiah also lays down conditions for divine protection and salvation, including faith ('If you do not stand firm in faith, you shall not stand at all', Isa. 7.9b) and righteous behaviour (1.19–20; 5.1–30; 33.14–16). Likewise, while Jeremiah can affirm that the Lord remains 'in Zion' (Jer. 8.19), he also inveighs against his compatriots who consider the Temple an automatic assurance of divine protection, arguing that such protection was contingent upon their own moral conduct (Jer. 7.1–15; 26.1–24). Yahweh's presence in Zion thus does not exclude the people from judgement; on the contrary, their ethical, social and cultic behaviour stands in stark contrast to the expectations of Yahweh, and thus its inhabitants will eventually be judged.

The Zion traditions also anticipate a time when the Lord will finally defeat all those nations which oppose Zion and the Lord's king or people. This will bring about two positive outcomes: the world will experience peace, and the nations will come to recognize the Lord as the ultimate power. For example, the author of Psalm 46 boldly asserts:

> Come, behold the works of the LORD;
>   see what desolations he has brought on the earth.
> He makes wars cease to the end of the earth;
>   he breaks the bow, and shatters the spear;
>   he burns the shields with fire.
> 'Be still, and know that I am God!
> I am exalted among the nations,
>   I am exalted in the earth.'
> The LORD of hosts is with us;
>   the God of Jacob is our refuge.   (Ps. 46.8–11)

The basis of this vision of peace is not pacifism, but rather the limitless scope of YHWH's triumph: his victory over the nations, his dominance over the world ensures that weapons will be futile. The recognition of YHWH's lordship is the basis of universal peace.   (Levenson, 1992: 1101)

This vision of peace centring on Zion seems to lie behind a number of prophetic texts, including Micah 4.1–4 (cf. Isa. 2.1–5) with its anticipation of a time when the nations will stream to the Lord's house, convert their weapons to farming implements and no longer engage in warfare.

3.3.3 David as the Lord's regent

According to Zion theology, Yahweh had not only chosen a place from which to rule but also a person and line who were involved in 'earthing' his rule. Throughout the Old Testament, the Davidic dynasty is described as being specifically chosen by the Lord to serve as his kings on earth.

Going deeper:
ELEVATED DESCRIPTIONS OF THE DAVIDIC KING

Just as God's earthly dwelling place, Zion, is described in elevated terms (see above), so too is his human king. For example, in Psalm 89.27 the Lord announces, 'I will make him [the Davidic king] the firstborn, the highest of the kings of the earth.' Psalm 2.7 describes the Israelite king as the 'son' of God. In this context, sonship language points to the unique status of the king, which he receives on the day of his enthronement. This status brings with it certain benefits: as son, the king is able to ask favours of God (Ps. 21.1–4) and receive divine aid in battle (Ps. 2.8–9).

The key text for understanding God's relationship to the Davidic kings is 2 Samuel 7. This chapter begins with David deciding to build a house for the ark shortly following his ascent to the throne. In an oracle given through the prophet Nathan, however, the Lord rejects David's offer and instead announces his choice of David and his 'house' (i.e. his dynastic line) as his human regents. Elsewhere in the Old Testament we discover that the Lord's commitment to David was sealed by an eternal covenant, which apparently reassured David that his dynastic line was secure, and that one of his descendants would always sit on the throne, even though God was free to punish or remove particular Davidic kings if they rebelled against him (cf. Pss. 78.70–72; 89.3–4, 19–37; 132.11–18) (Roberts, 2009: 987).[13]

The privileged position which the Davidic king enjoyed brought with it certain responsibilities. For example, the king was required to build and care for the Lord's Temple (2 Sam. 7.13).[14] Furthermore, the king was expected to

---

[13] For further discussion of the Davidic Covenant, see Williamson, 2007: 120–45.

[14] For further discussion of the king's role in the religious life of the nation, including the construction and maintenance of sanctuaries, see Chalmers, 2012: 89–97.

participate in Yahweh's work of establishing stability and justice throughout his kingdom. Thus, in Psalm 72.1–4 the psalmist pleads:

> Give the king your justice, O God,
>   and your righteousness to a king's son.
> May he judge your people with righteousness,
>   and your poor with justice.
> May the mountains yield prosperity for the people,
>   and the hills, in righteousness.
> May he defend the cause of the poor of the people,
>   give deliverance to the needy,
>   and crush the oppressor.

Since the Great King, Yahweh, was righteous and just (Pss. 89.14; 99.4), it was expected that his earthly regent would be involved in executing righteousness and justice as well (1 Kings 10.9).

The different elements of the Zion tradition became the basis for much of Israel's messianic and eschatological expectations even before Judah's exile but with increasing frequency thereafter. While one may have expected significant, calamitous events such as the fall of Jerusalem, the destruction of the Temple and the loss of the Davidic dynasty to lead to the 'death' of this ideology, this was clearly not the case. Instead, the tradition was transformed: the ideals remained, but hopes for their fulfilment were projected into the future.[15] For example, the failure of the various Davidic kings to live up to the high ideals associated with their office seems to have spurred the prophets not to reject Davidic kingship outright but rather to look forward to the arrival of a new king from the line of David who would reign with perfect justice and righteousness. Likewise, even though Jerusalem and the Temple lay in ruins, the prophets looked forward to a time when the Temple would be rebuilt, the city glorified and the nations stream to Zion to pay homage and tribute to the Lord, and to have their disputes settled by him. Speaking of the amazing work the Lord is about to do, the prophet Haggai announces:

> For thus says the LORD of hosts: Once again, in a little while, I will shake the heavens and the earth and the sea and the dry land; and I will shake all the nations, so that the treasure of all nations shall come, and I will fill this house with splendour, says the LORD of hosts. The silver is mine, and the gold is mine, says the LORD of hosts. The latter splendour of this house shall be greater than the former, says the LORD of hosts; and in this place I will give prosperity, says the LORD of hosts. (Hag. 2.6–9; cf. Isa. 2.2–4; Jer. 3.17)

In this way, one can see how the Zion traditions played an important role in providing the basic building blocks from which key elements of the prophetic hope were ultimately constructed.

---

[15] To put it another way, the traditional elements were now understood as envisioning future rather than present realities.

3.4 Guidelines for analysing the theological world of the prophets

The prophets did not live and speak in a vacuum. Nor were they creating their messages out of thin air. They were part of a broader conceptual and intellectual world, and their messages were shaped by and drew upon this. In particular, they were sensitive to the traditions that were present within their culture, as well as the cultures of the people around them.

According to Tate, 'Writers can exercise no alternative but to express themselves in the conceptual and ideological categories of their own time' (2008: 44). In fact, communication is only possible because the author and audience share a common frame of reference, a common way of viewing the world and a shared body of knowledge. The existence of such a framework means that authors can take certain things for granted, assuming their audience will 'get' what they are trying to say without needing to spell everything out. For example, where I teach in South Australia I can say someone is a 'crow eater' and most of my students will automatically understand that I am referring to a person who comes from the state of South Australia (popular tradition suggests that some of the state's early settlers were so short of food they ended up eating crows!). For those who do not share this frame of reference, however, my statement will be incomprehensible and may lead to all sorts of confusion. It is the same for our reading of the prophets. If we wish to hear their writings well, we need to familiarize ourselves with their conceptual framework and the knowledge they assumed. Or as Steck more technically puts it: 'One could speak of the aura of unrealized resonances in the formulation about which the exegete must later inquire and determine if he/she wants to participate in the original understanding of a text' (1995: 127).

In order to achieve this, I suggest a three-stage approach to interpretation which is based on a form of analysis known as tradition criticism.[16] Tradition criticism essentially enquires into what an author presumes, intends and insinuates through the use of traditional language (Steck, 1995: 139).

3.4.1 Identify loaded words or phrases

Traditions are often evoked simply through the use of a key word or phrase. These words or phrases are 'loaded' in the sense that they carry a weight of meaning or overtones, which the prophet assumed his or her audience would appreciate. It is perhaps helpful to conceive of these terms as 'shorthand' or code. Their mere mention would have triggered off a wealth of associations in the minds of the original hearers.

A modern example of a loaded phrase is '9/11'. Contemporary readers are well aware that this is more than simply a day in September. The phrase carries numerous associations and overtones (including, for example, the fall of the Twin Towers in New York, religious terrorism and significant loss of

---

[16] For a fuller discussion of tradition criticism, see Steck, 1995: 127–49; Rast, 1972.

life) that a modern author could reasonably expect his or her audience to grasp automatically. Of course, if the readers did not recognize this reference then it is entirely possible that they would not understand, or misconstrue, what the author was trying to say.

The prophets contain a wealth of loaded words and phrases. A few examples include:

> I looked on the earth, and lo, it was *waste and void*;
>   and to the heavens, and they had no light.
>   (Jer. 4.23)

Here Jeremiah evokes creation traditions (cf. Gen. 1.2) in order to describe the almost complete destruction which is about to overtake the nation. The prophet uses hyperbole to suggest that the impending conflict will lead to the end of the world and a return to primordial nothingness.

> This is like the *days of Noah* to me:
>   Just as I swore that the *waters of Noah*
>   would never again go over the earth,
> so I have sworn that I will not be angry with you
>   and will not rebuke you.   (Isa. 54.9)

In this passage the prophet recalls traditions associated with Noah and the flood, especially the Lord's promise that he would never again send a flood to destroy the earth (Gen. 9.8–17), as a means of emphasizing the significance and assuredness of the transition from judgement to salvation which the people are about to experience.

> I will set up over them one shepherd, my servant *David*, and he shall feed them:
> he shall feed them and be their shepherd.   (Ezek. 34.23)

Here the prophet harks back to traditions associated with the Davidic king (especially 2 Sam. 7) as a means of describing the ideal, future ruler whom God will appoint over his people.

Each of these passages evokes associations that we need to explore when doing our exegetical work if we wish to appreciate more fully what the prophet was trying to communicate.

3.4.2 Identify and explore which traditional element(s) the prophet is evoking

Tradition complexes are usually multidimensional, and the prophet may wish to evoke only part of these. For example, the phrase 'chariot and horse' (Isa. 43.17) may be associated with the exodus tradition in general, but it is specifically linked with the Egyptian pursuit of the Hebrews and the events at the Sea of Reeds (see Fig. 3.6).

An interesting example of the prophetic use of multidimensional traditions is Isaiah 1.9–10, with these verses drawing on different ideas commonly associated with Sodom and Gomorrah. In verse 9 Sodom and Gomorrah are used

Figure 3.6 Egyptian chariot and horses. Image of Ramses II storming the Hittite fortress of Dapur (Da-pu-ru); from a mural in his temple at Thebes

From the *Nordisk Familjebok*, vol. 6, Stockholm: Aktiebolaget Familjebokens Förlag, 1907. Wikimedia Commons.

as a means of emphasizing the *utter destruction* that the Lord could have inflicted on Israel had he been so inclined. In verse 10, on the other hand, the two cities are used in order to emphasize the *deep wickedness* of the people of Israel.

Going deeper:
OLD TESTAMENT THEOLOGICAL DICTIONARIES

The key resource for exploring loaded words or phrases is a theological dictionary. Unlike standard dictionaries (or lexicons) which tend to be quite restricted in the definitions they provide, theological dictionaries usually include extended discussions of the use and meaning of theologically significant words. The two best examples are: Botterweck, G., H. Ringgren and H-J. Fabry (eds), *Theological Dictionary of the Old Testament*, 15 vols (commonly abbreviated *TDOT*), and VanGemeren, W. (gen. ed.), *New International Dictionary of Old Testament Theology and Exegesis*, 5 vols (*NIDOTTE*). The articles in *TDOT* are written from a critical perspective, tend to be highly detailed (often including extensive discussions of ancient Near Eastern cognate terms), and assume some knowledge of Hebrew on the part of their readers. The articles in *NIDOTTE*, on the other hand, mainly come from evangelical scholars, and are written for those who have little or no knowledge of the Hebrew language, and who may not require quite the depth of discussion found in *TDOT* (e.g. some pastors, undergraduate students).

There is a variety of resources to help you explore the different traditional elements utilized by the prophets. A **concordance** lists other occurrences of the key word or phrase; an analysis of these will give you some idea of how the word or phrase is commonly employed in the biblical text. **Bible dictionaries** may contain discussions of the meaning of the key word or phrase and identify important occurrences in the Old Testament. **Theological dictionaries** focus on the meaning of the underlying Hebrew (or Aramaic) words and usually contain more detail than comparable entries in a standard Bible dictionary, but may require some original-language knowledge. Other valuable resources include **Old Testament theologies** (such as those written by Goldingay, Brueggemann, and Waltke), and **histories of Israelite religion** (see, for example, Preuss and Chalmers).

Going deeper:
PROPHETIC USES OF ANCIENT NEAR EASTERN TRADITIONS

We need to be aware that the prophets, like the Old Testament authors in general, did not draw solely from distinctly Israelite traditions. They could also utilize broader ancient Near Eastern traditions in order to convey their message. The interpreter of the prophetic writings, therefore, needs to develop a working knowledge of the conceptual world not just of Israel but of the ancient Near East as a whole.

A good example of the Old Testament authors' use of ancient Near Eastern concepts is the application to Yahweh of language and imagery commonly associated with other deities. For example, the description of Yahweh as a 'gracious God and merciful, slow to anger, and abounding in steadfast love' (Jonah 4.2; cf. Exod. 34.6) resembles one of the epithets of El, the head of the Canaanite pantheon (see Fig. 3.7), who is described as 'the benevolent, good-natured' one.[*] Such comparative analysis has pointed to a complex process of both convergence and differentiation in the biblical portrayal of Yahweh (i.e. Yahweh is depicted in ways that are both similar to and different from other ancient Near Eastern gods and goddesses).[†]

Critical appropriation of ancient Near Eastern traditions is also seen in the various descriptions of Yahweh battling and triumphing over the forces of chaos, often associated with the waters/sea, which we encounter both in the prophets and the book of Psalms. Isaiah 27.1 is an interesting example: 'On that day the LORD with his cruel and great and strong sword will punish Leviathan the fleeing serpent, Leviathan the twisting serpent, and he will kill the dragon that is in the sea.' This passage highlights an important dynamic: ancient Near Eastern traditions are not just borrowed by the Old Testament authors; they are transformed. According to the common ancient Near Eastern conception, the battle between the deity and the forces of chaos took place in the past, and was usually connected

---

[*] For further details see Chalmers, 2012: 104–7.
[†] The language of 'convergence' and 'differentiation' is taken from Smith, 2002. Smith's work is essential reading for anyone interested in the relationship of Yahweh to other ancient Near Eastern deities.

with creation of the heavens and earth (for further discussion see 3.3.1 above). In Isaiah 27, however, the battle is pushed into the future to highlight Yahweh's ultimate and final defeat of all the forces which oppose him.

For further discussion of the conceptual world of the ancient Near East and its relevance for understanding the Old Testament, see Walton, 2006.

Figure 3.7 Stele from Ugarit depicting an individual (perhaps a king or chief priest) presenting an offering to an enthroned god, probably El

My drawing, based on C. Schaeffer, 'Fouilles de Ras Shamra-Ugarit: Huitième campagne (printemps 1936)', *Syria* 18/2 (1937): 128–9, pl. and fig. 1.

3.4.3 Identify how the prophet uses and develops the tradition

This final step involves assessing how the prophet employs and possibly adjusts the traditional material to suit his or her purpose(s). According to Steck (1995: 145–6), the prophets could approach this material in one of three ways:

1 The prophet could *conform* to tradition: in this case, the prophet evokes or appeals to the tradition without significantly developing or altering this. Such use of the traditional material may be a means of establishing the veracity and/or authority of what the prophet is trying to communicate, as he or she is essentially drawing on well-established and generally accepted ideas.

    An example of this practice is Amos' citation of exodus and wilderness traditions in 2.10. This is part of the prophet's larger attempt to contrast the Lord's faithfulness to Israel (Amos 2.9–11) with the sin of the people

(2.6–8, 12), thereby providing a basis for his announcement of imminent judgement (2.13–16).

2 The prophet could *continue* the tradition: in this case, the prophet operates within the basic framework of the tradition but may extend or apply this in new ways or to new situations. Here we are dealing with a recontextualization or reactualization of the tradition rather than a simple quotation or citation.

An example of this practice is Deutero-Isaiah's use of the exodus tradition. The prophet takes up old ideas and images associated with Israel's deliverance from Egypt and uses these as a means of describing new events he discerns in the imminent future. This tradition thus forms the basis and starting point for his own unique message. Perhaps the best example of this practice is Isaiah 43.14–21, especially verses 16–19:

> Thus says the LORD,
>   who makes a way in the sea,
>   a path in the mighty waters,
> who brings out chariot and horse,
>   army and warrior;
> they lie down, they cannot rise,
>   they are extinguished, quenched like a wick:
> Do not remember the former things,
>   or consider the things of old.
> I am about to do a new thing;
>   now it springs forth, do you not perceive it?
> I will make a way in the wilderness
>   and rivers in the desert.

This passage is dripping with exodus language and imagery ('a way in the sea', 'chariot and horse', 'way in the wilderness'), but here the reference is not to the deliverance of Hebrew slaves from their bondage in Egypt but the return of God's people from their exile in Babylon. The prophet's proclamation is rooted in an understanding of the older divine work in history and is in essential continuity with this, but these traditions have been 'opened up' as a way of framing and explaining the prophet's expectations for God's future work of salvation (Rast, 1972: 66–7).

3 The prophet could *change* the tradition: 'the author changes traditional concepts or conceptual contexts by deviating from accents or formulations, or by changing the train of thought even to the point of reversing the tradition' (Steck, 1995: 146). In so doing the prophet has essentially transformed the tradition; he or she has given the tradition a personal, distinct twist such that there is little continuity with its regular meaning and usage.

Such changes are often important for discerning the prophet's message and, therefore, it is worth paying close attention to them when doing our exegetical work. In this context we need to consider three related questions:

(a) How has the traditional material been changed?
(b) What is the significance of these alterations?
(c) Why has the prophet altered the tradition in this way? What is his purpose?

Amos 5.16–17 provides a good example of the prophet altering traditional material.[17] Here the prophet announces:

> Therefore thus says the LORD, the God of hosts, the Lord:
> In all the squares there shall be wailing;
>   and in all the streets they shall say, 'Alas! alas!'
> They shall call the farmers to mourning,
>   and those skilled in lamentation, to wailing;
> in all the vineyards there shall be wailing,
>   for I will pass through the midst of you,
>
> says the LORD.

Verse 17 contains an allusion to the exodus tradition and, in particular, the events associated with the first Passover. The prophet, however, has transformed this tradition dramatically: instead of the Lord 'passing over' the Israelites in salvation, he will now 'pass through the midst' of them in judgement. The prophet is making the point that the coming judgement of Israel is going to be terrible and horrific – as terrible and horrific as God's final plague on the Egyptians, the death of the firstborn. The prophet may also be working with a second tradition here: the reference to 'passing through *the midst*' appears to link back to the Lord's presence among the people as they journeyed from Egypt to the promised land (cf. Exod. 25.8; 29.45–46; Lev. 15.31; Num. 14.14, etc.). Whereas previously the Lord's presence was, more often than not, a source of blessing and protection, here it is something to be feared, a source of affliction.

A key problem we need to be aware of when performing this kind of analysis is the tendency to assume that the prophet is directly responsible for any and all variations in the traditional material. It needs to be recognized, however, that Old Testament traditions are, by their very nature, quite fluid; we are not dealing with completely fixed and static ideas or concepts. Instead, Broyles speaks of the dynamic nature of Old Testament traditions – 'through Israel's changing circumstances and fluctuating faithfulness, and through Yahweh's progressive revelation, traditions developed, sometimes through evolution and sometimes through revolution' (2001b: 164). Hence, the 'variations' we encounter can be attributed to a number of different factors. They may be a result of the work of the prophet, but they may also stem from the divergences within the tradition itself (e.g. Jeremiah's characterization of the wilderness period as a time when Israel loved and followed the Lord (2.2) appears to reflect a positive view of the wilderness wanderings which is also seen in Hosea 2.15) or broader historical changes in the concept (Steck, 1995: 137).

---

[17] Another example is Isaiah 29.1–4. Here the prophet describes how Yahweh will besiege 'Ariel' (i.e. Jerusalem) at the head of the armies of the nations. This is a reversal of the standard motif of Yahweh defending Jerusalem and attacking Israel's foes.

3.5 Summary

In this chapter we have considered two key Israelite traditions which form the background to and provide the basic shape for much of the prophetic proclamation. Essentially, these traditions centre on the two great mountains in Israel's story: Mt Sinai and Mt Zion. Sinai traditions are concerned with the relationship between the Lord (who is portrayed as a mighty suzerain) and the people of Israel (who are portrayed as the Lord's vassal), with a particular focus on Israel's responsibilities in the light of this relationship (as laid out in the various covenant stipulations, i.e. the laws). These traditions help us grasp the basis for and nature of the indictments the Lord brings against Israel through the prophets, and the accompanying announcements of divine judgement (and eventually restoration) which embody the covenantal curses and blessings. Zion traditions, on the other hand, focus on the relationship between the Lord (who is portrayed as the Great King) and the Davidic king (who is portrayed as the Lord's regent), and emphasize the importance of Zion/Jerusalem as the divine and human kings' imperial capital. These traditions help us grasp the centrality of Jerusalem and the Temple within some prophetic thought (especially Isaiah), the indictments brought against Israel's kings (who often fail to live up to the expectations associated with their position as the Lord's regent) and the hopes attached to the Davidic monarchy (that one day a king would come who would reign with perfect righteousness and justice). The attentive reader needs to grasp how these – and other – traditions are incorporated and transformed by the prophets if he or she wishes to hear the prophetic message in all its depth and fullness.

Further reading

Discussions of Old Testament traditions and tradition criticism

Broyles, C. (ed.). *Interpreting the Old Testament: A Guide for Exegesis*. Grand Rapids: Baker, 2001 (esp. chs 1 and 5).

Gravett, S., K. Bohmbach, F. Greifenhagen and D. Polaski. *An Introduction to the Hebrew Bible: A Thematic Approach*. Louisville: WJKP, 2008 (esp. ch. 11).

Levenson, J. *Sinai and Zion: An Entry into the Jewish Bible*. New York: HarperCollins, 1987.

Rast, W. *Tradition History and the Old Testament*, GBSOTS. Philadelphia: Fortress, 1972.

Williamson, P. *Sealed with an Oath: Covenant in God's Unfolding Purpose*, NSBT 23. Downers Grove: InterVarsity Press, 2007.

Discussions of the theology of individual prophetic books

Gowan, D. *Theology of the Prophetic Books: The Death and Resurrection of Israel*. Louisville: WJKP, 1998.

Hays, J. D. *The Message of the Prophets: A Survey of the Prophetic and Apocalyptic Books of the Old Testament*. Grand Rapids: Zondervan, 2010.

McConville, G. *Exploring the Old Testament, vol. 4: Prophets*. London: SPCK, 2002.

4

The rhetorical world of the prophets

4.1 Introduction

The third world we need to consider when interpreting the prophets is their rhetorical world. Before we can discuss this, however, it is worth clarifying exactly what we mean by 'rhetoric' and 'rhetorical'. The word 'rhetoric' does not have positive connotations for many people. 'That's just rhetoric' implies that something may sound good, but is, in fact, untrue or lacking in substance. 'Engaging in rhetoric' is something we accuse our politicians of doing when we are sceptical of what they are saying. In everyday usage 'rhetoric' is a (negatively) weighted term, implying that something is high on style but low on meaning.

In scholarly discourse, however, 'rhetoric' and 'rhetorical' are used in a much more neutral fashion. Here, 'rhetoric' is commonly understood as:

1 the study of the technique of using language effectively;
2 the art of using speech to persuade, influence or please; oratory.[1]

When considering the rhetorical world of the prophets, therefore, we are enquiring as to how the prophets effectively used language to persuade and influence their audience, and how they shaped their material to communicate their message in a compelling fashion. In short, while focusing on the theological world of the prophets concentrates our attention on *what* the prophets said (i.e. the content of their message), considering their rhetorical world asks *how* they communicated (i.e. their method). Our analysis of the rhetorical world of the prophets will need to take place on two levels:

1 We will consider the *rhetorical structure* of the individual prophetic units of speech (including the use of forms);
2 We will analyse the *rhetorical features* of Hebrew poetry and the various literary and rhetorical devices which the prophets could employ.

4.2 Rhetorical structure

One of the most important elements of interpreting the prophetic literature involves identifying the structure of the textual unit under consideration. In fact, the very first thing I think we need to do when we encounter a new

---

[1] These definitions are taken from the *Collins English Dictionary – Complete and Unabridged 10th Edition* (<http://dictionary.reference.com/browse/rhetoric?s=t>, accessed 16 December 2013).

93

textual unit is to analyse its structure. If we can figure this out, if we can identify the individual elements of the unit and how these work together as a whole, then we are well on the way to understanding its message.

Analysing the rhetorical structure of a textual unit is a three-stage process:

4.2.1 Identifying the units within the passage

This stage involves identifying the self-contained textual units and establishing their extent, i.e. where they begin and end. Just as you would not start or stop reading a book halfway through, you need to make sure that you are dealing with entire oracles.

Going deeper:
ORGANIZING PRINCIPLES IN THE PROPHETIC BOOKS

Much of the prophetic material has been brought together in what may, at first, seem like random or haphazard fashion. In reality, however, there is usually some logic behind the location of a given unit. For example, there may be thematic considerations in play (a good example of this is the collection 'concerning the drought' in Jer. 14.1—15.4).* Alternatively, chronological ordering may be important; this is certainly the case for books such as Haggai and Zechariah. Other possible 'organizing principles' include a movement from judgement to salvation (a number of books, including Ezekiel and Zephaniah, witness a broad movement from judgement against Israel, to judgement of the nations, to consolation and restoration of Israel) or the use of link words or catchwords (e.g. the prophecy against Israel's leaders beginning in Isa. 1.10 has been placed following 1.9 due to the reference to Sodom and Gomorrah in both verses).

---

* There are also collections within Jeremiah which relate to the 'house of the king of Judah' (21.11—23.8), 'the prophets' (23.9–40) and judgement on foreign nations (e.g. Moab in ch. 48).

This step is essential because, as I argued in Chapter 1, the prophetic books are essentially anthologies. Words which the prophets spoke at various times and in various places have been written down and brought together, usually without any divisions in the text to indicate where one unit ends and another begins. Unfortunately, modern verse, chapter and paragraph divisions may not be helpful in this regard as they are the product of much later scholarship (there are no chapter and verse divisions in the original Hebrew text) and thus should be approached with caution.[2] For example, some chapter divisions break apart material which belongs together (e.g. there should be no major division between Amos 1.15 and 2.1; the first two chapters of Amos form

---

[2] The chapter divisions, for example, are largely the work of Bishop Stephen Langton (early thirteenth century AD), while the verses are associated with Robert Estienne (or Stephanus) (early to mid-sixteenth century AD).

one continuous series of oracles which announce God's judgement first against the surrounding nations, and then against Israel itself) or bring together material which was originally separate (e.g. Amos 4 is actually made up of at least three distinct units: a word against the rich women of Samaria (vv. 1–3), a parody of priestly instruction/exhortation (vv. 4–5) and a historical review of divine judgements linked with an announcement of imminent judgement (vv. 6–13)).[3]

Admittedly, some prophetic books, or parts thereof, do have a more clearly defined structure with more clearly delineated textual units. For example, in Haggai and the early chapters of Zechariah each prophecy is dated, and sometimes provided with a narrative introduction (see, for example, Hag. 1.1; 2.1–2, 10, 20). This is also the case for some sections of the major prophets (esp. Jer. 25—35; Ezekiel). It needs to be emphasized, however, that this practice is not common (little information is provided, for example, in Jer. 1—24); such clear delineation is the exception rather than the norm.

How then do we go about identifying the individual textual units within a passage? As Stuart (2009: 5) points out, the primary ally of the interpreter is usually common sense. After working through the passage carefully and closely, you will often have a gut feeling for where one unit ends and another begins. In addition, there may be certain features, or 'tells', present in the text to help guide your thinking (Deppe, 2011: 1). These include:

1 *Prophetic formulas.* These may be used to mark out where a unit begins and ends. Common examples include 'And the word of the Lord came to . . .', 'Hear the word of the Lord . . .' (these usually mark out the beginning of a unit), 'Thus says the Lord' and 'declares the Lord' (which are often used to conclude the unit). For example, Amos 4.1–3 begins with the announcement: '*Hear this word*, you cows of Bashan . . .' and concludes with the declaration '. . . and you shall be flung out into Harmon, *says the Lord*.'
2 *Change in content.* Each textual unit will usually have content which is self-contained, cohesive and meaningful. Thus, one should pay 'meticulous attention to all details in the unit under discussion and to their combining to yield a coherent message' (Rofé, 1997: 47). A change in content is often a good indicator that you are dealing with a new unit. For example, in Amos 4 the prophet shifts from discussing the sacrificial and offering system of Israel (vv. 4–5) to a historical account of the judgements God has enacted on Israel (vv. 6ff.), suggesting that a new unit has begun.
3 *Change in speaker.* Sometimes a change of speaker may indicate the start of a new unit. It is, therefore, worth considering who is speaking: the Lord, the prophet or the people.[4] For example, in Amos 7.1 we see a shift from the Lord speaking (note the 'I' of 6.14) to the prophet.

---

[3] Some scholars divide up this final section, suggesting it ends at v. 11 or 12.

[4] Technically, the correct question is 'Who is speaking on behalf of whom?': does the prophet speak in the name of the Lord, does he utter his own words or is he speaking on behalf of the community? (Rofé, 1997: 56–7).

4 *A new form.* Units can also be isolated by attention to known prophetic forms (for a discussion of the most common forms, see below). For example, Amos 4.4–5 is an example of the priestly instruction/exhortation form, albeit with some significant modifications. This form would usually begin with the priest addressing the people with plural imperatives, setting forth instructions concerning the cultic ritual to be performed at the shrine, and conclude with a declaratory formula which would provide the basis for the cultic activity ('for I am Yahweh your God' or a reference to Yahweh's will or pleasure in the cult) (Mays, 1969: 74). The presence of such elements – even though Amos has refashioned them with biting sarcasm – allows us to identify where the textual unit begins and ends.

Going deeper:
AMOS' USE OF THE PRIESTLY INSTRUCTION FORM

In Amos 4.4–5 the prophet adapts a priestly instruction/exhortation form. Two key changes are particularly noticeable: (i) the prophet is inviting the people to come to the cultic sites of Bethel and Gilgal *to sin* (v. 4), and (ii) the prophet concludes by locating such religious activity in the will of the people ('for so you love to do, O people of Israel!', v. 5) rather than the will of God. Such alterations would have created a 'shocking dissonance' (Mays, 1969: 74) for Amos' original hearers, and would have been a powerful way of both capturing his audience's attention and conveying his confronting message.

It needs to be emphasized, however, that none of these features is a perfect guide in and of itself. We may, for example, find prophetic formulas *within* a unit, rather than at its beginning or end. For example, 'thus says the Lord' is often found at a significant point of transition within a prophecy of judgement, marking the transition from indictment to announcement of divine judgement, rather than at its conclusion (for more details, see below). Content is also not a fail-safe tell. As suggested above, one of the organizing principles for prophetic books is that units that focused on a similar topic or theme were often located together. Thus, a new textual unit may have begun, even though the basic content has not changed. It is therefore necessary to apply these criteria cautiously and to look for the presence of multiple diagnostic features.

Once you have attempted to identify the unit(s), it is worth consulting some resources, especially commentaries and modern English translations, to check your work and refine your thinking. Such resources can function as a useful guide – by examining your selection against theirs you should be able to tell whether or not your own tentative identification of a unit's boundaries has a solid basis. If you are starting a unit where no scholar has begun or finishing where no scholar has ended, you need to be careful. While you may have discovered something new, this is unlikely to be the case. It is worth being aware, however, that decisions regarding boundaries and the structure of a passage are sometimes subjective, and thus there may be debate among the scholars themselves. If this is the case, it is up to you to decide which, in your opinion, is the best option.

4.2.2 Identifying the structure of the unit(s)

Once you have identified the textual unit(s), your next goal is to analyse the structure of the one(s) you wish to focus on. Analysing the structure of a unit essentially involves trying to figure out the internal dynamics of the text: what are the identifiable subsections and how do these work together to create an effective piece of communication?

Identifying the subsections of the unit is usually not too difficult. 'To explain the thought flow of a given passage often requires paying attention to and thinking carefully about the significance of the obvious' (Klein, Blomberg and Hubbard, 2004: 264). In fact, many of the features we have discussed for identifying distinct units within a passage apply here as well. Tells that may mark the presence of subsections include:

1 *Conjunctions.* Essentially, conjunctions are joining or linking words; they connect blocks of material (words, phrases or clauses) together. There are two main types of conjunctions which are particularly significant for interpreting the prophets: temporal or chronological (e.g. 'while', 'after') and logical (e.g. 'but', 'however'). Although small in size, conjunctions often play an important role in regulating the flow and direction of a text's argument (Klein, Blomberg and Hubbard, 2004: 270). For example, the logical conjunction 'therefore' is often used to mark an important transition from the prophet indicting the people to announcing divine judgement (because the people have committed sin *x*, 'therefore' they will experience divine judgement *y*; see Amos 3.11 below).

2 *Change in speaker/addressee.* As suggested above, a change in speaker can be an important structural feature and may be used to indicate a new subsection. This is also true for a change in addressee. In Amos 3 the first subsection (v. 9a) is delineated by the fact that the addressee is the prophet, whereas in the second (v. 9b) it is (the strongholds of) Ashdod and Egypt.[5]

3 *Change in content.* A change in the basic theme/idea of the unit may indicate a new subsection. For example, the shift from the prophet declaring the people's sin in Amos 3.10 to announcing God's intention to act in judgement in 3.11 marks out a new subsection.

4 *Forms.* The various prophetic forms tend to follow common patterns, with well-defined subsections (for more details see below).

5 *Repetition.* This is the most common structural device in Hebrew literature, and its presence may point to the existence of subsections. For example,

---

[5] While the MT reads 'Ashdod', the LXX has 'Assyria'. 'Ashdod' is more likely to be correct as this is the more difficult reading and Ashdod is also mentioned in 1.8, whereas we find no other references to Assyria in the book.

Amos 4.6–13 presents a litany of divine judgements on the northern kingdom. Each of these is marked out by an introductory declaration in which the Lord announces his performance of a negative action against the people ('I did x to you ...') and concludes with the repeated phrase 'yet you did not return to me, says the LORD.'

A number of the above features can be seen in Amos 3.9–11 (see Fig. 4.1):

Proclaim to the strongholds in Ashdod, and to the strongholds in the land of Egypt, and say,	*Introduction and identification of witnesses (the addressee is the prophet)*
'Assemble yourselves on Mount Samaria, and see what great tumults are within it, and what oppressions are in its midst.'	*Call to witnesses (the addressee is the strongholds of Ashdod and Egypt)*
They do not know how to do right, says the LORD, those who store up violence and robbery in their strongholds.	*Accusation (change in content)* *Prophetic formula* *Identification of the accused with implied accusation*
Therefore, thus says the Lord GOD: An adversary shall surround the land, and strip you of your defence; and your strongholds shall be plundered.	*Logical conjunction* *Prophetic formula* *Announcement of judgement / punishment (change in content)*

4.2.3 Identifying the purpose/nature/significance of the subsections

Once the subsections have been identified, it is worth considering the purpose of each of these. In order to do this you should focus on both the function and the content of each subsection. Write out a short summary of each subsection in which you identify what the prophet was trying to achieve (for an example see Amos 3.9–11 above). Because these summaries focus on the purpose (the why) of each subsection, they should not be unique, but be capable of being applied to multiple passages.

These summaries should help you identify the flow of thought, or 'movement', of your unit. 'The *structure* of the passage refers to its parts, its main divisions and subdivisions, while the *movement* of a passage refers to the progression of the text, through those parts, from beginning to end' (Gorman, 2001: 79). In pre-exilic prophetic texts a movement from some form of introduction, to an indictment which highlights the people's sins, followed by an announcement of judgement which has been brought about as a consequence of the sins (and often reflects these in some way) is commonly utilized. Additional typical movements are found within the various prophetic forms.

Figure 4.1 The Assyrians destroying and burning the city of Khamanu in Elam. Note the soldiers removing the precious goods from the city

Hall, H. *Babylonian and Assyrian Sculpture in the British Museum*. Paris: Les Éditions G. van Oest, 1928.

4.2.4 Prophetic forms

**Going deeper:
FORM AND GENRE**

Although some scholars use the terms 'form' and 'genre' interchangeably, I am distinguishing between the two, with form a subset of genre. Genre refers to the broader category of literature (e.g. narrative, law, poetry), while form refers to different types of narratives or poems. For example, the book of Psalms contains a number of well-known forms, including the lament, song of thanksgiving, and hymn. The scholarly analysis of forms is referred to as 'form criticism'. For a fuller discussion of form criticism, see the classic work Tucker, 1971.

In your attempts to identify the units, subsections and movement of a prophetic text, it is worth keeping in mind that the prophets could employ a wide variety of forms to convey their message. These were not necessarily unique creations on the part of the prophets, but were often drawn from the daily life and communal traditions of the people. 'It is difficult to conceive of a type of speech or a sphere of Israelite life which is not at least reflected in the words of the prophets' (Tucker, 1971: 31). The various forms that the prophets utilize usually possess specific content, a certain structure and a fixed purpose, although some variability is to be expected with regards to any given occurrence.[6] The following represents a brief summary of some of the key prophetic forms:

4.2.4.1 *Prophecy of judgement*[7]

This is the most characteristic form of the prophetic literature, and particularly dominates the pre-exilic prophets. Here the prophet announces imminent or future divine judgement on an individual, group or entire nation. It usually consists of three key elements:

1 *Indictment.* Here the prophet states the accusation or the problem(s)/situation(s) that has occasioned the message of judgement. The accusation can be quite general in nature (e.g. a generic reference to the people's sin) or more specific (highlighting particularly problematic practices), and may begin with 'Because . . .' or an interrogative. In this section, the prophet provides the reasons for the announcement of judgement which will shortly follow.
2 *Messenger speech.* The announcement of judgement (element 3) will often be preceded by the messenger formula 'Thus says the Lord . . .' (which itself is often introduced by the logical conjunction 'Therefore . . .'). This serves to authenticate the divine origins of the word.
3 *Announcement of judgement.* The prophet describes, often in graphic detail, the divine judgement that is to come. This regularly involves some form

---

[6] Form critics also argue that the individual forms share a common life-setting (or *Sitz-im-Leben*). The settings, which included the cult, legal institutions, family life etc., had recurrent situations which required a distinctive form of speech. For example, the family often experienced death and needed a way to express their sense of grief and loss, hence the dirge was utilized. These life-settings were the place in which such forms were created and developed.

[7] This form is also referred to as 'prophecy of disaster', 'prophetic judgement speech' and 'prophecies of punishment' in the secondary literature.

of 'poetic justice', i.e. the judgement reflects the nature of the indictment levelled against the people (e.g. because the rich have oppressed the poor, they will be oppressed).

Sometimes this form may begin with an introductory call to hear (e.g. 'Hear this word . . . !') or a divine commission ('Go, prophesy . . .'). A good example of this form is Amos 7.16–17:

Now therefore hear the word of the LORD.	*Introductory call to hear*
You [i.e. Amaziah] say, 'Do not prophesy against Israel, and do not preach against the house of Isaac.'	*Indictment/ accusation*
Therefore, thus says the LORD: 'Your wife shall become a prostitute in the city, and your sons and your daughters shall fall by the sword, and your land shall be parcelled out by line; you yourself shall die in an unclean land, and Israel shall surely go into exile away from its land.'	*Messenger speech Announcement of judgement*

A particular type of the prophecy of judgement is the *woe oracle* or *woe speech*. 'The woe oracle commonly appears in prophetic literature as a means to criticize specific actions and attitudes of people, and to announce punishment against them' (Sweeney, 2005: 41). The characteristic feature of this form is that it begins with the opening cry of dismay 'Woe . . . !' (Heb. *hôy* sometimes translated 'Alas' or 'Ah'), usually followed by one or more participles (or nouns) which describe the recipients of the oracle. This opening 'woe' plus participle combination often functions as an implicit indictment, highlighting the evil deeds that the addressees of the oracle have committed, and thus the reason they are worthy of woe. Such oracles may appear individually or in a series. A good example is Isaiah 5.8–10:

Ah, you who join house to house, who add field to field, until there is room for no one but you, and you are left to live alone in the midst of the land!	*Declaration of woe (with implicit indictment)*
The LORD of hosts has sworn in my hearing: Surely many houses shall be desolate, large and beautiful houses, without inhabitant. For ten acres of vineyard shall yield but one bath, and a homer of seed shall yield a mere ephah.	*Divine oath Announcement of judgement*

Figure 4.2 Relief of Egyptian funeral procession from the tomb of Merymery. Note the portrayal of people engaged in various activities associated with mourning

© Rob Koopmans / Wikimedia Commons.

The exact origin of the woe speech form within Israelite society remains a point of debate among scholars. Some associate this with funeral or mourning practices (see Fig. 4.2), while others have attempted to connect it with wisdom teaching. Either way, such speech would have had a powerful impact: 'To the Israelite *woe* signified tragedy and imminent sorrow' (Osborne, 2006: 268).

4.2.4.2 Prophecy of salvation[8]

This form becomes more common in the later prophets, especially from the period of the exile onwards. The prophecy of salvation is basically the positive counterpart to the prophecy of judgement: instead of announcing imminent disaster, the prophet proclaims future restoration, salvation and blessing.

The structure of the prophecy of salvation resembles the prophecy of judgement; however, the section detailing the reasons why God is about to act in salvation (the equivalent of the indictment) is often omitted or, if it is included, tends to focus on God's grace, mercy or love rather than the good deeds or piety of the people. Israel has not done anything to warrant its salvation, but God has decided to act anyway.

---

[8] This form is also known as the 'prophecy of blessing', 'prophecy of deliverance' or 'announcement of well-being'.

When later in the midst of dark judgement the entirely new promise of salvation breaks forth, it in no way happens because of a new approach of the people to Yahweh; on the contrary, salvation breaks forth as Yahweh's free gift in spite of the hopelessness and unbelief of the people. (Wolff, 1987: 24)

The final section, the announcement of salvation, is usually quite long and may include a proclamation of deliverance, a description of divine blessing (which may involve material prosperity, the restoration of the nation, agricultural abundance, etc.) and/or a reassurance of God's presence. Amos 9.13–15 is a good example of this form:

The time is surely coming,	*Time notation*
says the LORD,	*Messenger formula*
when the one who ploughs shall overtake the one who reaps,	*Announcement*
and the treader of grapes the one who sows the seed;	*of salvation/*
the mountains shall drip sweet wine,	*blessing*
and all the hills shall flow with it.	
I will restore the fortunes of my people Israel,	
and they shall rebuild the ruined cities and inhabit them;	
they shall plant vineyards and drink their wine,	
and they shall make gardens and eat their fruit.	
I will plant them upon their land,	
and they shall never again be plucked up	
out of the land that I have given them,	
says the LORD your God.	*Messenger formula*

4.2.4.3 Prophetic disputation speech

The disputation speech form was probably drawn from the wisdom sphere where it was employed as an instructional device (Sweeney, 2005: 41). It is designed to persuade the prophet's audience to accept a certain idea or perspective, and often includes argument against an alternative (often the popular!) point of view. Key features may include the following:

1 The prophet quotes the viewpoint/thesis he or she wishes to reject;
2 The prophet refutes the viewpoint/thesis and proposes another in its place;
3 The prophet employs rhetorical questions to involve the audience;
4 The prophet concludes with a lesson.

Unlike most of the forms we have examined so far, the prophet does not always quote the direct voice of God but may instead speak in his or her own terms (e.g. Isa. 40.27–31). Isaiah 49.14–26, especially verses 14–18, provides a good example of this form (note how the ordering of elements is not fixed):

But Zion said, 'The LORD has forsaken me,   *Quotation*
my Lord has forgotten me.'   *of rejected*
    viewpoint

Can a woman forget her nursing child,   *Rhetorical*
or show no compassion for the child of her womb?   *questions*
Even these may forget,   *Alternative*
yet I will not forget you.   *viewpoint*
See, I have inscribed you on the palms of my hands;
your walls are continually before me.
Your builders outdo your destroyers,
and those who laid you waste go away from you.
Lift up your eyes all around and see;
they all gather, they come to you.
As I live, says the LORD,
you shall put all of them on like an ornament,
and like a bride you shall bind them on ...
I will make your oppressors eat their own flesh,
and they shall be drunk with their own blood as with wine.
Then all flesh shall know   *Lesson*
that I am the LORD your Saviour,
and your Redeemer, the Mighty One of Jacob.

4.2.4.4 Prophetic lawsuit

As suggested above, Israel's prophets drew their forms from a wide variety of social settings. This included ancient Israel's legal practices. In a number of passages the prophet speaks as if a party (Israel, the nations, the gods of the nations) were on trial accused of a crime. Yahweh plays the dual role of prosecutor and judge, presenting a case against the defendant and announcing its fate. Such texts sometimes charge Israel with breach of the covenant, and for this reason the form has been referred to as a 'covenant lawsuit'.

The key identifying features of this form include the use of legal terminology (e.g. 'case', 'accusation' and 'indictment'[9]) and references to trial procedures such as:

1 a summons to the divine court;
2 the calling of witnesses – these can be human nations or Creation itself (i.e. 'heaven and earth');
3 a charge/accusation;
4 a speech by the defendant;
5 the citation of evidence that proves the guilt of the defendant;
6 a verdict describing the judgement or sentence which is due.

---

[9] The Hebrew term *ríb* is often employed.

It needs to be recognized, however, that not all these elements may be (explicitly) present in a given text, and that their ordering may vary. Hosea 4.1–3 is an example of this form:

Hear the word of the LORD, O people of Israel;	*Call to hear*
for the LORD has an indictment against the inhabitants	*Announcement*
of the land.	*of indictment*
There is no faithfulness or loyalty,	*Accusation*
and no knowledge of God in the land.	
Swearing, lying, and murder,	*Evidence*
and stealing and adultery break out;	
bloodshed follows bloodshed.	
Therefore the land mourns,	*Verdict*
and all who live in it languish;	
together with the wild animals	
and the birds of the air,	
even the fish of the sea are perishing.	

4.2.4.5 Prophetic vision report

Going deeper:
THE DIFFERENT KINDS OF VISION REPORTS

Klein, Blomberg and Hubbard (2004: 369) have identified three main types of vision reports on the basis of variations in content and style. These include:

1 *The 'oracle vision'.* This features a question-and-answer dialogue between Yahweh and the prophet about something the prophet sees and which provides the occasion for the oracle (e.g. Jer. 24; cf. 1.11–14; Amos 7.7–8; 8.1–2; Zech. 5.1–4).
2 *The 'dramatic word vision'.* This depicts a scene in heaven that portends some future event on earth which the prophet presumably is to announce (e.g. Amos 7.1–6; Jer. 38.21–22).
3 *The 'revelatory-mystery vision'.* Here an angelic interpreter dialogues with the prophet about the (often strange) symbolic imagery he sees (e.g. Zech. 2.1–4; cf. 4.1–6; Dan. 8; 10—12). The purpose of the conversation is to reveal the veiled secrets of God's future plans. This form of vision is particularly found in prophetic-apocalyptic sections of the Old Testament (for further details, see Chapter 5).

As we have seen in Chapter 1, one of the key titles for the Old Testament prophets was 'seers' (Heb. *rō'eh* or *ḥōzeh*), probably because they sometimes received divine revelation through visions (see Fig. 4.3 overleaf). The prophetic books contain a number of first-person narrative vision reports which describe such experiences. These characteristically include:

Figure 4.3 'Isaiah's vision of the destruction of Babylon (Isa. 13)'
from Doré's *English Bible*

Engraving from G. Doré, *The Holy Bible, with Illustrations by Gustave Doré*. London and New York: Cassell,
Petter and Galpin, 1866–70. Wikimedia Commons.

1 an introduction to the vision with a reference to the prophet 'seeing' (or
   being shown);
2 a transitional expression (usually 'and behold . . .') which introduces the
   vision proper;
3 a description of the vision itself.

A series of such vision reports is found in Amos 7—8, for example at 7.4–6.

This is what the Lord GOD showed me:	*Introduction to the vision*
[lit. and behold]	*Transitional expression*
the Lord GOD was calling for a shower of fire, and it	*Description of the vision*
devoured the great deep and was eating up the land.	
Then I said,	*Response of the prophet*
'O Lord GOD, cease, I beg you!	*Prophetic intercession*
How can Jacob stand?	
He is so small!'	
The LORD relented concerning this;	*Divine response to*
'This also shall not be,'	*intercession*
said the Lord GOD.	

Figure 4.4 'So shall the king of Assyria lead away the Egyptians as captives and the Ethiopians as exiles, both the young and the old, naked and barefoot, with buttocks uncovered, to the shame of Egypt' (Isa. 20.4). Relief depicting the Assyrians attacking a walled Egyptian city. A number of prisoners with their hands tied, and some with shackled feet, are being led away (c.667 BC)

Hall, H. *Babylonian and Assyrian Sculpture in the British Museum*. Paris: Les Éditions G. van Oest, 1928.

4.2.4.6 Symbolic action report

The prophetic books also contain a number of first- and third-person narratives which describe an act performed by the prophet designed to communicate Yahweh's word.[10] This prophetic form typically consists of three elements:

1 a divine command to perform a certain action;
2 a (brief) report of the prophet performing the action;
3 an interpretation of the meaning/significance of the action, provided by the Lord.

The following example comes from Isaiah 20.1–6 (see Fig. 4.4):

---

[10] For a fuller discussion of the nature and significance of these symbolic actions, see Chapter 1.

In the year that the commander-in-chief, who was sent by King Sargon of Assyria, came to Ashdod and fought against it and took it – at that time the LORD had spoken to Isaiah son of Amoz, saying,	*Time notation and introduction to report*
'Go, and loose the sackcloth from your loins and take your sandals off your feet', and he had done so, walking naked and barefoot.	*Divine command Report of prophetic performance*
Then the LORD said, 'Just as my servant Isaiah has walked naked and barefoot for three years as a sign and a portent against Egypt and Ethiopia, so shall the king of Assyria lead away the Egyptians as captives and the Ethiopians as exiles, both the young and the old, naked and barefoot, with buttocks uncovered, to the shame of Egypt. And they shall be dismayed and confounded because of Ethiopia their hope and of Egypt their boast. In that day the inhabitants of this coastland will say, 'See, this is what has happened to those in whom we hoped and to whom we fled for help and deliverance from the king of Assyria! And we, how shall we escape?'	*Interpretation of the significance of the action*

4.2.5 Potential problems to avoid

The main problem we need to avoid when considering forms is that of imposing an 'ideal' form on the unit under examination. While proper identification of the form of a unit may help refine your understanding of its key elements and structure, you need to be careful not to let the known *typical* features of the form dominate or dictate the way you analyse the *specific* features of the unit (Stuart, 2009: 120). The prophets may have borrowed many of their forms from the world around them but they were hardly slaves to a set of fixed patterns which had to be followed – the prophets felt free to modify and rework the forms to serve their own distinct purposes; elements could be added, reordered or omitted altogether. Thus, while knowledge of the various prophetic forms can function as a useful guide for identifying the structure and movement of a given unit, we need to be careful that we do not automatically and rigidly impose the standard formulaic pattern onto the text.

4.3 Rhetorical features

An analysis of the rhetorical world of the prophets also requires us to consider the various ways the prophets used language, especially poetic language, to convey their message in a persuasive fashion. In order to achieve this, we need to consider first what makes Hebrew poetry in general compelling and persuasive. Given that the majority of Old Testament prophecy is written as poetry, it is essential that we develop some awareness of how this genre communicates meaning.[11] Second, we need to consider the various literary and rhetorical devices the prophets employed and the way these work if we wish to exegete their writings faithfully.

4.3.1 Parallelism

The dominant feature of much modern (especially popular) English poetry is end-of-line rhyming. The Old Testament equivalent of this is parallelism.

As its name implies, parallelism involves two or three lines of poetry (sometimes referred to as colon (sing.) or cola (pl.)) set in parallel with each other. There will be some kind of correspondence between the elements of both lines.[12] Often, the second line will essentially restate the thought of the first line using different words (this is sometimes referred to as 'synonymous parallelism'). For example, in Amos 1.2a the prophet declares:

> The LORD roars from Zion,
>   and utters his voice from Jerusalem . . .

Here the phrase 'utters his voice' repeats the idea of 'roaring', while Zion (which technically refers to the Temple mount) is essentially used as a synonym for Jerusalem. On other occasions, the second line will contrast with the first (sometimes referred to as 'antithetical parallelism'), add to the first (referred to as 'climactic parallelism') or complete or expand the idea of the first (referred to as 'synthetic parallelism').[13]

Generally speaking, parallelism adds a dynamism or richness to what the prophet is trying to say. 'Parallelism focuses the message on itself but its vision is binocular. Like human vision it superimposes two slightly different views of the same object and from their convergences it produces a sense of depth' (Adele Berlin, cited in Klein, Blomberg and Hubbard, 2004: 284). It also forces the reader to slow down and focus his or her attention on the thought the prophet is trying to convey, thereby helping to increase the impact of the statement.

Some people place a lot of emphasis on identifying and classifying the different types of parallelism that are present in a poem or prophecy. In my opinion, this is not essential.[14] What *is* important, however, is realizing that

---

[11] Although less common, prose elements are found in the prophetic books and may be employed as part of a conscious literary and rhetorical strategy (Petersen, 1997: 32–3). For further discussion see Alter, 1987: 137–9.

[12] 'Parallelism consists of two, sometimes three, successive colons in which an idea is restated, embellished, or contrasted by repetition' (Lundbom, 2010: 159). The parallel lines may interrelate grammatically, lexically and semantically, numerically and phonologically. For further details, see LeMon and Strawn, 2008: 510–12.

[13] For a fuller discussion of the different types of parallelism, see Klein, Blomberg and Hubbard, 2004: 289–97.

[14] One could argue that the differences in the labelling of the various forms of parallelism in the secondary sources make precise identification a questionable task anyway.

Hebrew poets communicate using multiple-line constructions and that the lines may be related in any number of different ways.

An awareness of the presence and nature of parallelism should help us avoid over-exegeting the text. A prophet usually does *not* try to say two different things or attempt to make two distinct points over two lines. Instead, he states or develops the one main idea in two different ways. Hence, another possible label for parallel cola is a 'thought couplet' (Ryken) in that the two lines together are designed to convey a single thought. Practically, this means that you will need to train your eye to read poetry in blocks of two (or three) lines, and then ask, 'What is the author saying over both lines?'

4.3.2 Imagery (including metaphors and similes)

Old Testament prophecy is full of vivid imagery. In fact, it is helpful to think of the Hebrew prophets as literary artists who paint graphic images of divine judgement and blessing, using words instead of brush strokes. Due to its prevalence and importance, the ability to interpret imagery is one of the most crucial skills for understanding the prophetic literature.

The use of imagery as a means of communication has been viewed with a certain degree of suspicion in the West. We generally prefer more scientific or propositional modes of discourse. Recent research into metaphors and metaphorical language, however, has shown that imagery is, in fact, a powerful way to communicate. Within the Old Testament prophets it serves three key functions:

1 *Imagery helps to make the abstract concrete.* Thus, it allows the prophets to talk about ideas which cannot be easily expressed and described through more propositional styles of discourse, e.g. the terrible severity of God's judgement, the wondrous abundance of God's blessing.
2 *Imagery engages the reader/hearer in a way that straight, didactic prose is unable to.* Good imagery encourages the reader to enter into and participate in what the author is saying; one can almost taste, smell or feel the message. Imagery is thus an affective mode of communication – it moves the audience on an emotional level, or, in the words of Fee and Stuart, it 'was addressed to the mind through the heart' (2003: 207).
3 *Imagery increases the memorability of concepts and ideas by painting visual pictures.* 'Metaphor and simile possess arresting strangeness that both captures a reader's initial attention and makes a statement memorable ... They force a reader to ponder or meditate on a statement. They contain a retarding element that resists immediate assimilation. Like the parallelism of biblical poetry, they require a reader to pause on a thought before moving on' (Ryken, 1992: 168).

Imagery is often conveyed through the use of metaphors or similes. While metaphors and similes are customarily distinguished, it is worth keeping in mind that there is, in fact, a great deal of overlap between them. Both are essentially based on comparing one thing with another; they suggest that A is somehow like B.

Technically speaking, a simile indicates that one thing (A) is 'like' another (B). For example, in Hosea 5.14 the Lord declares:

> For I will be *like* a lion to Ephraim,
>   and *like* a young lion to the house of Judah.

Alternatively, the key word 'as' may be used. Thus, Hosea 8.8 announces:

> Israel is swallowed up;
>   now they are among the nations
>   *as* a useless vessel.

Metaphors, on the other hand, claim that one thing (A) 'is' another (B), with the key words 'like' or 'as' omitted. Here the two items are linked more directly via a form of the verb 'to be' ('was', 'is', 'will be', etc.). Good examples of metaphors are found in the following two verses:

> The grass withers, the flower fades,
>   when the breath of the LORD blows upon it;
> surely the people *are* grass.   (Isa. 40.7)

> The officials within [the city]
>   *are* roaring lions;
> its judges *are* evening wolves
>   that leave nothing until the morning.
>   (Zeph. 3.3)

Going deeper:
A BROADER DEFINITION OF METAPHORS

It is worth recognizing that some scholars adopt a less restrictive definition for metaphors and metaphorical language than that proposed here (i.e. 'A is B'). For example, Sandy argues that 'in metaphorical language, nonfigurative words with definitions that are generally well known are used to refer figuratively to something outside the purview of accepted lexical referents' (2002: 63). 'Let's talk turkey' is an example of metaphorical language according to this definition because it utilizes a non-figurative word ('turkey') in a way which we would not find listed in a standard dictionary entry. Essentially, we encounter a metaphor whenever we are asked to understand and experience one kind of thing in terms of another (Sandy, 2002: 74).

The key to interpreting simile and metaphors is to figure out the significance of the B item, i.e. the item which is being used figuratively. It is worth developing an awareness of two features:

1 the idea(s) that the item conjured up in the minds of the original Israelite hearers;
2 the emotion(s) that the item evoked in the original hearers of the prophecy.

It may help to visualize the image the prophet is creating as part of this process. Let the picture sink into your consciousness and come alive in your imagination. 'The more sensory and concrete these images become in our imagination, the richer will be our experience of poetry' (Ryken, 1992: 161). Such imaginative engagement, however, should not take the place of histori-cal research. Sandy has emphasized the cultural dimensions of metaphorical language, arguing that metaphors are often understandable only because the audience shares a common cultural background with the author: 'Metaphor as a function of community means that hearers who are not a part of the com-munity will be less prepared to identify and understand metaphors' (2002: 65). It is therefore incumbent on contemporary interpreters to do their historical work – to identify whether a statement is metaphorical or not[15] and to find out what the image meant and evoked *to the original audience* – as they attempt to bridge the significant language and cultural barriers between the biblical and twenty-first-century worlds.

> ### Going deeper:
> ### RICOEUR AND METAPHORS
>
> Paul Ricoeur, the twentieth-century French philosopher, recognized that metaphors are 'both a thinking and a seeing' (1978: 147). The 'seeing' occurs when the image conjures up a picture in the reader's mind's eye. The 'thinking' takes place when we trace the logic of the connection between the two items and transfer the mean-ing from one to the other (Ryken, 1992: 167).

Once the interpreter has developed an awareness of the ideas and emotions associated with the B item, he or she then needs to identify the point(s) of contact with A, the thing with which it is being compared. In what way(s) are the two things alike? Why has the author chosen this particular item to represent the other?

The interpretation of some of the prophetic images may seem relatively straightforward. This is often because such images essentially 'mean' the same thing now as they did back then. For example, the lion symbolizes aggression, power and strength both in the modern Western and biblical contexts. The meaning of other images, however, will be less obvious. For example, Hosea

---

[15] Sandy (2002: 189–94) provides 12 criteria for identifying whether a statement of prophecy is meta-phoric or not.

describes Ephraim (i.e. the northern kingdom) as an 'unturned cake' (Hos. 7.8, my translation) and a 'trained heifer that loved to thresh' (Hos. 10.11). In these cases, you may need to consult some resources, including Bible dictionaries. A particularly valuable text for interpreting metaphors and similes is L. Ryken, J. Wilhoit and T. Longman III, 1998. This dictionary provides good discussions of the images, symbols, motifs, metaphors, figures of speech and literary patterns which are found in the Bible.

Of course, we need to be careful that we do not assume that we know what an image 'means' simply because we are aware of the ideas it conjures up today. The meaning of an image in its ancient context may well be different from its contemporary meaning; the significance of images often changes from time to time and from place to place. For example, the image of the lion would have evoked a strong emotional response of fear in the ancient Israelites as it was not uncommon for travellers through the wilderness to be taken by wild animals, such as lions. It is possible that lions do not evoke the same feeling of fear in modern Westerners (or at least not to the same extent) as the only lions we are likely to see are tamed or in captivity, safely behind bars.

The final step in interpreting metaphors and similes is to determine their function within their context.[16] In other words, why did the prophet use this particular image for his argument? How did it contribute to the message he desired to convey? What effect did he hope to achieve? 'Only when the function of what is being said is clear can the language be understood' (Sandy, 2002: 80). For example, the leonine similes of Hosea 5.14 serve to emphasize the inescapable, violent and overwhelming divine judgement which is about to come on the northern kingdom.

As with parallelism, the main mistake we need to avoid when interpreting imagery is the tendency to over-exegete. By this I mean that we can press imagery too far – we may attempt to draw meaning from an image that the prophet did not intend. There are usually only a limited number of contact points between the image and the thing with which it is associated. Like words, images may have a range of meanings (a semantic range), but they will usually only mean one thing in a given context. For example, the image of a lamb may suggest gentleness or innocence, but in Isaiah 40.11 it is employed to emphasize the helplessness and dependence of the people. Your goal is to decide which aspect(s) of the B item are central to the simile or metaphor and not to go beyond this.

4.3.3 Literary and rhetorical devices

In addition to the rhetorical features of Hebrew poetry discussed above, the prophets employed a variety of literary and rhetorical devices (also referred

---

[16] It is not uncommon for a prophet to string together a series of similes or metaphors. This is usually done in order to heighten the emotional impact the author is trying to create. Each simile or metaphor is like the brush strokes of a painter on a canvas: the more there are, the richer the portrait. Generally speaking, however, the images will work together to make a central point.

to as 'figures of speech') to convey their message. I will concentrate on the ones which are most significant for exegesis.[17]

The first two literary devices, *metonymy* and *synecdoche*, both involve substitution. *Metonymy* involves the substitution of a word or idea for one closely associated with it (Klein, Blomberg and Hubbard, 2004: 313). The substitute serves as a verbal 'stand in', representing the other. For example, in Amos 7.9 (NIV) the Lord declares, 'The high places of *Isaac* will be destroyed and the sanctuaries of Israel will be ruined'. In this instance, 'Isaac' is functioning metonymically – Isaac is an important ancestor of Israel so the name has become another way of indicating the kingdom of Israel. Another example is Jeremiah 50.6: 'My people have been lost sheep; their shepherds have led them astray, turning them away on the *mountains*; from mountain to hill they have gone, they have forgotten their fold.' Here the initial reference to 'mountains' in fact denotes illicit pagan worship practices which are taking place on the mountains (cf. Hos. 4.3; Deut. 12.2).

Synecdoche is similar to metonymy; in fact, it is a specific type of metonymy. In this case, a part of something serves to represent the whole idea or item. The author focuses 'attention on something specific as a symbol of something larger' (Klein, Blomberg and Hubbard, 2004: 313). A common example in the prophets is the use of 'Ephraim' (the name of the largest of the ten northern tribes) or 'Samaria' (the capital of the northern kingdom from the reign of Omri onwards) to refer to the entire northern kingdom. Another example is the use of 'sword' to evoke an entire army.

The next two rhetorical devices, *irony* and *sarcasm*, are also closely related. *Irony* occurs when 'a writer says the opposite of what he means' (Klein, Blomberg and Hubbard, 2004: 314). In other words, it can be a way of telling the truth by stating an untruth. For example, in Amos 4.4 the prophet declares:

> Come to Bethel – and transgress;
>   to Gilgal – and multiply transgression;
> bring your sacrifices every morning,
>   your tithes every three days . . .

Here Amos appears to be inviting the people to go to Bethel and Gilgal, ancient sites which had become corrupted as places of Israelite worship by the prophet's time, to offer their sacrifices. His goal, however, is the opposite of his literal statement (he does not, in fact, want the people to go to these places and sin) and hence he is employing irony. Irony can become *sarcasm* when the speaker deliberately mocks or pokes fun at the object of his or her words (Klein, Blomberg and Hubbard, 2004: 314). The Lord employs sarcasm in his taunts of the idols/false gods which are found in the second half of the book of Isaiah (e.g. 41.21–24, especially vv. 22–23).

---

[17] For a fuller discussion of the various figures of speech and rhetorical devices the prophets employed along with numerous examples, see Lundbom, 2010: 167–207.

Prophecy, like biblical poetry in general, is highly affective; it is written to address and move the reader on not just an intellectual but also an emotional level. A key way in which emotion is conveyed in biblical poetry is via imagery. It is also expressed through the use of *hyperbole*. Essentially, hyperbole is 'conscious exaggeration for the sake of effect' (Ryken, 1992: 177). For example, in the statement 'She cried for days' the time has been exaggerated in order to emphasize the severity of the person's distress. Hyperbole is used by the prophets to express strong feeling or emotion (especially divine anger or love) and is frequently employed when the speaker is trying to be persuasive by creating an impact.[18]

> **Have you considered?**
> **HYPERBOLE AND PROPHETIC DESCRIPTIONS OF SALVATION**
>
> While it may be easy to accept that descriptions of divine judgement are hyperbolic, we need to consider that descriptions of divine salvation may also be exaggerated. It seems reasonable to postulate that if the prophets used hyperbole to emphasize the divine wrath against sin, so too would they use hyperbole to emphasize God's lavish love for his people and his desire to save and bless them. Thus, we need to be careful how literally we interpret the numerous prophetic references to agricultural prosperity, increased influence, material wealth and the transformation of nature which the prophets anticipate God bringing about. For example, Amos declares:
>
> > The time is surely coming, says the LORD,
> > when the one who ploughs shall overtake the one who reaps,
> > and the treader of grapes the one who sows the seed;
> > the mountains shall drip sweet wine,
> > and all the hills shall flow with it.   (Amos 9.13; cf. Joel 3.18)
>
> While these things are certainly possible for an all-powerful God, we should be open to the possibility that such statements were not intended to be taken at face value but are instead designed to make the point that God will surely save his people and provide for them abundantly.

Good examples of hyperbole include Jeremiah 17.4 and 25.9. In the former passage, the Lord declares:

> By your own act you shall lose the heritage that I gave you, and I will make you serve your enemies in a land that you do not know, *for in my anger a fire is kindled that shall burn for ever.*

---

[18] 'Hyperboles, in effect, stretch the truth in order to increase the impact of the words' (Sandy, 2002: 41).

In the latter, the Lord announces:

> I am going to send for all the tribes of the north ... even for King Nebuchadrezzar of Babylon, my servant, and I will bring them against this land and its inhabitants, and against all these nations around; *I will utterly destroy them*, and make them an object of horror and of hissing, *and an everlasting disgrace*.

In both these passages, the Hebrew adverb *'ôlām* (translated as 'for ever' and 'everlasting' respectively) is being used hyperbolically.[19] The Lord is not stating that his anger will literally burn for ever, but he is making the point that he is *extremely* angry with the people, and that his judgement will be severe. Likewise, the Lord does not intend to wipe out the people completely (how could they be an object of horror and of hissing if they were no more?), but he does plan to bring terrible and overwhelming judgement against them.[20]

The main problem we face when interpreting hyperbole is that we may not, in fact, recognize that we are dealing with it! We may think that the prophet's word should be taken literally instead of realizing that he has deliberately exaggerated the situation. This is a serious mistake; the person who thinks I literally have 1,000 kilograms of assignments when I declare, 'I've got a tonne of homework', has completely missed what I am trying to say. One way to overcome this potential problem is to ensure that we do not get too caught up in the details of the prophecy and instead focus on its overall message: ask, 'What is the big idea of this prophecy?', 'What is the prophet trying to achieve through the use of such extreme language?'

The final two literary devices, *hendiadys* and *merism*, are also closely related. In both, a single idea is expressed using two (or more) words and it is the total concept (not the individual elements in isolation) which is important. *Hendiadys* (from the Greek meaning 'one through two') occurs when two or three terms, usually joined by the conjunction 'and', are used together to convey one single but complex idea or concept (Watson, 2005: 324–5).[21] For example, Isaiah 51.3b describes the consequences of God comforting Zion; this involves the city experiencing 'joyful gladness' (not 'joy *and* gladness' as suggested by the NRSV). Similarly, Jeremiah 3.2 contains a description of Israel's spiritual adultery. The reference to the people's 'whoring and wickedness' (NRSV) does not imply two separate actions (as if they have committed wicked crimes on top of being unfaithful) but instead emphasizes their 'wicked whoring'.

---

[19] For a thoughtful discussion of the use of the term 'for ever' in biblical prophecy, see Sandy, 2002: 98–101.

[20] Hyperbole is also frequently used to describe military forces. See, for example, the description of the Assyrian army in Isa. 5.26–30. This depiction 'transforms the Assyrian hosts into a virtually supernatural agency' (Alter, 1987: 152).

[21] More precisely, the two nouns mutually define each other (Klein, Blomberg and Hubbard, 2004: 302 n.98).

> **Going deeper:**
> **HENDIADYS IN ISAIAH 51.19**
>
> The clearest indication that two Hebrew words could combine to form a single unit,
> namely hendiadys, occurs in Isaiah 51.19 (Watson, 2005: 326). Here the prophet
> announces, 'These *two* things have befallen you [i.e. Jerusalem] . . .', but in fact
> goes on to list *four* ('devastation and destruction, famine and sword'). In this case,
> the four words are two examples of hendiadys: 'devastation and destruction' =
> 'destructive devastation', and 'famine and sword' = 'stabbing starvation'.

**Figure 4.5 'Then shall the young women rejoice in the dance'
(Jer. 31.13). Terracotta figurine of a woman holding a drum from
the pre-exilic period**

© Israel Antiquities Authority / Israeli National Maritime Museum.

A *merism* involves the prophet mentioning the extremes of some category
in order to portray it as a totality (Klein et al., 2004: 302).[22] In other words,
the prophet will cite two opposites in order to imply everything in between
them. For example, in Isaiah 65.17 the Lord declares, 'For I am about to

---

[22] A merism is also a form of synecdoche, in that part of the idea/concept is used to evoke the
whole.

create new heavens and a new earth', which implies that he will transform Creation as a whole. Likewise, in Jeremiah 31.13 the Lord promises, 'Then shall the young women rejoice in the dance, and the young men and the old shall be merry', to suggest that everyone will celebrate God's redemption of Israel (see Fig. 4.5). As we have already seen in the case of hendiadys, it is not *just* the individual elements themselves that matter but what they amount to together, as a unit (Watson, 2005: 321). Thus, when interpreting hendiadyses and merisms you need to ask yourself: what is the meaning that is conveyed by these elements as a whole? What is the idea the author is trying to convey through using these two terms?

4.4 Summary

When we speak of the rhetorical world of the prophets, we are essentially concerned with considering how the prophets sought to make their speech effective and persuasive. An appreciation of this world leads us to analyse the text on two levels. First, we investigate the *rhetorical structure* of the text, which involves identifying the various units within a passage, and then focusing on the structure and movement within these. This process can be aided by a knowledge of the various forms the prophets commonly employed (e.g. prophecy of judgement, prophecy of salvation, prophetic disputation speech, prophetic lawsuit, prophetic vision reports, symbolic action reports). Second, it involves considering the *rhetorical features* of Hebrew poetry (such as parallelism and the use of images) as well as appreciating the literary and rhetorical devices the prophets utilized (including metonymy and synecdoche, irony and sarcasm, hyperbole, merism and hendiadys).

The problem with approaching prophetic rhetoric in this fashion, however, is that it may cause us to think that interpretation is something we do from a distance, as analytical, detached outsiders. It may lead us to conceptualize the ideal interpreter as a laboratory scientist who stares down at the text through a microscope, but who essentially remains separated from the object he or she is studying. I would argue, however, that such an approach and image is ultimately less than satisfactory in and of itself, for the majority of prophecy is poetry, and poetry calls the interpreter to engage with and be moved by the world the poet is creating.

> Poetry is not just a set of techniques for saying impressively what could be said otherwise. Rather, it is a particular way of imagining the world ... [with] its own logic, its own ways of making connections and engendering implications.
> (Alter, 1987: 151)

Thus, the picture of the interpreter as a laboratory scientist needs to be balanced by the recognition that good interpreters are also contemplatives – people who spend time ruminating over the text, who enter into the experience of the text and allow the text to capture their imagination. Unless both emphases (analysis and contemplative engagement) are at work, it is unlikely that the interpreter will fully grasp the prophets' message for their original audience, and by extension, their audience today.

Further reading

Klein, W., C. Blomberg and R. Hubbard, *Introduction to Biblical Interpretation*, rev. edn. Nashville: Thomas Nelson, 2004.

Rofé, A. *Introduction to the Prophetic Literature*, BS 21. Sheffield: Sheffield Academic Press, 1997.

Ryken, L. *Words of Delight: A Literary Introduction to the Bible*, 2nd edn. Grand Rapids: Baker, 1992.

Sandy, D. B. *Plowshares and Pruning Hooks: Rethinking the Language of Biblical Prophecy and Apocalyptic*. Downers Grove: IVP, 2002.

Sweeney, M. *The Prophetic Literature*, IBT. Nashville: Abingdon, 2005.

Watson, W. *Classical Hebrew Poetry: A Guide to Its Techniques*. T&T Clark Biblical Languages. London: T&T Clark, 2005.

5

From prophecy to apocalyptic

5.1 Introduction

In a number of the later prophetic texts such as Daniel, Zechariah and Malachi a change appears to take place.[1] Whereas the prophets usually envisage God acting in salvation or judgement within history, these passages seem to anticipate a climactic and decisive intervention of God that brings history (at least as we know it) to a definitive culminating point. Whereas the prophets characteristically hear God's word and receive visions of a relatively mundane, everyday nature (e.g. Amos sees a plumb-line and basket of fruit, Amos 7.7–9; 8.1–2), these books contain dramatic visions of great beasts emerging out of the sea (Dan 7.2–7), of angels wrestling with evil powers (Dan. 10), of cosmic upheaval (Isa. 24.18–20; Ezek. 38.19–22). Whereas the prophets normally focus on earthly events, these passages are just as concerned with what takes place in the heavenlies. In short, there seems to be a shift in both the form and content of these texts. This has led many scholars to suggest that we are encountering the emergence of a new genre – apocalyptic – and it is to these passages that we turn in this chapter.

Apocalyptic texts often evoke two different kinds of response. Some people become obsessed with the material, and use it as the basis for all kinds of speculation regarding the significance of contemporary events in the Middle East, and the (usually imminent) end of the world. Thus, Daniel 11 is frequently taken to anticipate a devastating war between the modern-day nations of Russia (the kingdom of the north) and Egypt (the kingdom of the south). Dozens of books and hundreds of internet sites are devoted to such sensational speculation. This kind of approach, however, is nothing new, having a long tradition in both Jewish and Christian circles.[2] The Qumran community believed that the visions in Daniel were about to be fulfilled in their day, Luther identified the Turks with the fourth beast of Daniel 7 and encouraged Christians to join in the eschatological battle against them, while in the USA William Miller decided on the basis of Daniel 8.14 that the world would end in 1843, with the so-called Millerite movement not collapsing until 1845!

---

[1] In this chapter I primarily focus on the apocalyptic material that is found in the Old Testament, and thus consideration of the book of Revelation will be kept to a minimum.

[2] For example, Josephus' hesitancy to discuss Dan. 2 in much detail seems to imply that he believed Rome to be the fourth empire (*Antiquities* 10.10.4 (10.210)). For a more detailed summary of the history of Danielic scholarship, including a discussion of Jewish perspectives, see the fine Introduction to Goldingay, 1989.

The other response (perhaps provoked by the excesses associated with the first) is to ignore these passages altogether. With their strange imagery, hyperbolic use of language, and graphic descriptions of God's judgement, not a few Christians have given up on ever understanding these texts and moved on to other books which, on the surface at least, appear to be more consistent with their existing theological beliefs and relevant to their contemporary situation. The relative neglect of these books is also not a new phenomenon; for example, Revelation was the only New Testament book for which Calvin did not produce a commentary.

In this chapter, I will explain how we can go about hearing the voice of God in these fascinating, but often confusing, passages without resorting to the excesses and speculation of the 'fanatics' or the disregard and neglect of those who choose largely to ignore them. But before we can do this, we need to deal with a few preliminary issues: what is apocalyptic and how is it different from prophecy, and where do we find apocalyptic texts?

5.2 What is apocalyptic and how is it different from prophecy?

It needs to be emphasized from the outset that prophecy and apocalyptic are not two completely distinct genres. Apocalyptic is essentially a subset of prophecy, and grows out of prophecy. It is prophecy with a special form and striking content, or, to put it more colloquially, it is 'prophecy on steroids'. In order to conceptualize the relationship between the genres, it is helpful to think of prophecy and apocalyptic as two ends of a spectrum upon which we can locate our Old Testament texts. Some texts will have more of the features we commonly associate with apocalyptic, whereas others will more closely resemble traditional prophecy.

Going deeper:
THE 'MIXED PARENTAGE' OF APOCALYPTIC

Following the lead of von Rad, Russell (1994: 33) has argued that apocalyptic is a child with 'mixed parentage': its mother is prophecy; its father is the wisdom tradition, especially mantic wisdom.* As is the case with any human family, the children of such a union may differ greatly from one another and will often take after one parent more than the other. Daniel, for example, is more prophetic in tone and content, in comparison to a text like the apocryphal *1 Enoch* which indulges in the kind of speculation that is also to be found in some of the wisdom writings of the period.

_____

* The influence of wisdom is seen, for example, in the tendency of some texts to list cosmological and meteorological phenomena, and to understand and categorize the various realms of Creation.

All the texts labelled apocalyptic can be located somewhere within the
triangle, combining elements of prophecy, wisdom and 'full-blown'
apocalyptic to different degrees

Defining apocalyptic is a notoriously tricky endeavour and has been the subject
of intense debate within biblical scholarship. The English word 'apocalyptic' is
based on the Greek word *apokalypsis* which means to 'reveal' or 'unveil' knowledge which had been previously hidden.[3] While this may point towards the
content of apocalyptic, these texts are also marked out by their distinctive *form*.
Grant Osborne has proposed a definition which we can use as the starting point
for our discussion:

> Apocalyptic entails the revelatory communication of heavenly secrets by an
> other-worldly being to a seer who presents the visions in a narrative framework;
> the visions guide readers into a transcendent reality that takes precedence over
> the current situation and encourages readers to persevere in the midst of their
> trials. The visions reverse normal experience by making the heavenly mysteries
> the real world and depicting the present crisis as a temporary, illusory situation.
> This is achieved via God's transforming the world for the faithful.
>
> (2006: 276)

It is worth unpacking this definition, drawing attention to a few of the key
ways in which apocalyptic texts differ from prophecy.[4]

5.2.1 Apocalyptic literature emphasizes a visionary mode of revelation

Prophecy is usually presented either as direct speech from God or as
visions from God. The book of Amos, for example, combines both these
elements: much of the book appears to consist of direct utterances from
God, while in chapters 7—9 the prophet describes a series of visions which

---

[3] The label 'apocalyptic' technically fits several different phenomena: it applies to a body of literature
(a genre), a particular type of religious imagination (a worldview) and to a specific sort of group
within society (a social entity) (Cook, 2003: 22). We will primarily restrict our discussion to the
first and second categories in this chapter. For a fuller discussion of apocalyptic social entities, see
Cook, 1995.

[4] Scholars often suggest that pseudonymity (i.e. the attribution of the work to a revered figure who did
not actually produce it) is also a key feature of apocalyptic texts; however, the presence of pseudonymity in the Old Testament is debated. For the conservative perspective on this issue, see Osborne,
2006: 280.

Figure 5.1 'Daniel's vision of the four beasts emerging out of the sea (Dan. 7)' from Doré's *English Bible*

Engraving from G. Doré, *The Holy Bible, with Illustrations by Gustave Doré*. London and New York: Cassell, Petter and Galpin, 1866–70. Wikimedia Commons.

focus on the coming judgement of Israel.[5] Although prophecy is generally poetic in form and employs sometimes striking imagery, this is regularly drawn from everyday life and/or the natural world (e.g. Hosea likens Israel to a 'senseless dove' (7.11) and an 'unturned cake' (7.8), my translations). Thus, the meaning of the various oracles is usually not too difficult to discern.

In apocalyptic, God reveals his previously hidden future plans usually through dreams or visions. Unlike the visions we find in the prophets, however, these are full of elaborate and, at times, strange and mysterious symbolism and/or numbers. Many of the dominant images of apocalyptic belong to the realm of fantasy or myth, or we encounter surreal, unnatural combinations. For example, Daniel 7 contains a vision of four great beasts, including a bear with tusks in its mouth and a lion with eagle's wings, coming out of the sea (see Fig. 5.1), while Daniel 8 describes a goat with a horn that grows as high as the host of heaven. The meaning and significance of these dreams and visions is thus often obscure; serious interpretive work is required.

---

[5] Prophets also often have visions of God in connection with their call (e.g. Isa. 6; Jer. 1; Ezek. 1—3).

5.2.2 In apocalyptic literature revelation is often mediated by a third party

In the prophetic literature, God directly reveals his will and word to the prophets. Jeremiah 23.18–19 suggests that the prophet stands in the council of God where he or she personally sees and hears the Lord's word which must be communicated to the people.

In apocalyptic, however, there is often a third party – usually an angel – whose role is to help the seer understand the strange and mysterious visions he is receiving. While the interpreting angel does not provide the revelation per se (God remains the source), he does help to mediate this in the sense that he makes it comprehensible to the seer. For example, in Zechariah 6.1–8 the seer perceives four chariots – one with red horses, another with black horses, the third with white horses and the last with dappled grey horses – coming out from between two mountains of bronze (see Fig. 5.2). The seer, however, is unsure of the significance of this vision, and thus asks the angel, 'What are these, my Lord?' to which the angel promptly provides an interpretation (vv. 5–8).

Going deeper:
THE ROLE OF THE ANGEL GABRIEL

The only interpreting angel who is named in the Old Testament is Gabriel. He appears in the book of Daniel where he explains the vision of the he-goat and the ram (8.16) and the prophecy of the 70 (weeks of) years (9.21). Gabriel also plays a revelatory role in the New Testament: he foretells the birth first of John the Baptist (Luke 1.19) and then of Jesus (Luke 1.26) (cf. *2 Enoch* 21 where the angel has similar words of encouragement for Enoch). The intertestamental literature, especially the books of *Enoch*, offers additional light on Gabriel's nature and role. In *1 Enoch* 9 he appears as one of the four archangels and is responsible, along with the other archangels, for interceding for the inhabitants of the earth. Other passages in *1 Enoch* suggest that he is in charge of 'paradise and the dragons and the cherubim' (20.2) and has a role to play in punishing the wicked (54.6), while the Qumran texts emphasize his militant role.

5.2.3 Apocalyptic texts often have a narrative framework and are literary compositions

As we have seen in Chapter 1, the prophetic books are anthologies – they consist of a series of originally independent oracles which were brought together to form larger collections, usually on the basis of shared content or other considerations. These oracles have been placed back to back with little to no narrative introduction. Narratives about the prophets themselves, especially the minor prophets, are also rare. The book of Amos, for example, contains just one narrative which runs for a total of eight verses (7.10–17),

Figure 5.2 'Zechariah's vision of four chariots (Zech. 6)' from Doré's
English Bible

Engraving from G. Doré, *The Holy Bible, with Illustrations by Gustave Doré*. London and New York: Cassell, Petter and Galpin, 1866–70. Wikimedia Commons.

while many of the other minor prophets have no narrative material at all. An apocalyptic text such as Daniel, on the other hand, is essentially structured as a narrative, with the various visions integrated into this broader narrative framework. Note, for example, the narrative material which is located between and helps to introduce the visions in chapters 8, 9, 10 and 11.

Furthermore, it is likely that the apocalyptic texts were originally written compositions, in contrast to prophecy which began life as a spoken word and was only recorded in writing at a later stage. For example, John of Patmos is instructed by the risen Lord to 'write what you have seen, what is, and what is to take place after this' (Rev. 1.19; cf. 1.11), and Daniel is explicitly described as writing down his dream (7.1). As a result, apocalypses tend to be more literary and complex, and thus require greater sophistication on the part of their interpreters.

5.2.4 Apocalyptic literature focuses on the end of history[6]

Prophecy is primarily (though not exclusively) concerned with God's actions within history. As discussed in Chapter 2, a significant portion of the prophetic writings focuses on God's imminent judgement of Israel and Judah (prophecies which were largely fulfilled by the events of 722 and 586 BC respectively), or anticipates God's impending act of salvation. The intervention of God, whether in judgement or salvation, usually takes place through either natural means (locusts, drought, etc.) or human agents. For example, God acts to judge the sin of the northern kingdom by raising up the Assyrians, while he liberates the Babylonian exiles by calling Cyrus of Persia. Essentially, God is indirectly involved in these events, in the sense that he acts through natural phenomena or the machinations of world empires.

The apocalypticists, however, tend to focus on a decisive, climactic act of God which will bring a violent, radical end to history as we know it, an end that would mean the triumph of good and the final judgement of evil. Furthermore, rather than work within human history, the apocalyptic God radically intervenes from outside it; the seers anticipate God's *direct* intervention in judgement and blessing (Klein, Blomberg and Hubbard, 2004: 385). For example, Isaiah 64.1 (NIV) implores God himself to 'rend the heavens and come down' – this is heaven invading the earth.

This final, great act of God will be cosmic in scope, embracing all nations and the entirety of Creation. In fact, a characteristic feature of the apocalyptic texts is their graphic descriptions of God's judgement on all the nations of the earth (cf. Joel 3.11–12; Zech. 12.1–4). For the righteous, however, these texts anticipate a golden age of peace and prosperity, with Isaiah 25.6–10 utilizing the image of a rich banquet to describe God's great act of salvation.

But it is not only humanity which is the object of God's activity in the apocalyptic texts. Isaiah 24.1 suggests that the Lord is about to 'lay waste the earth and make it desolate' (cf. 24.3, 19–20), while in 24.21–23 God

---

[6] It should be recognized that apocalyptic language and imagery does not always describe 'end times' events. Dan. 7, for example, appears to be referring to various historical human empires (although their precise identity remains a point of scholarly dispute). Similarly, Sandy has argued that Zephaniah's language of cosmic catastrophe (e.g. Zeph. 1.2–3) was really about the Babylonian destruction of Jerusalem; he did not see down the road as far as the end times (private correspondence). Thus, while apocalyptic texts as a whole tend to be concerned with God's climactic, decisive intervention in history, we need to be careful of automatically assuming that this is the case for every occasion where apocalyptic language is used.

will act in judgement on 'the host of heaven in heaven ...Then the moon will be abashed and the sun ashamed'. If the rest of Creation is subject to God's judgement, however, it will also be caught up in his work of salvation and renewal. Thus, Isaiah 65.17 anticipates God creating new heavens and a new earth, and Joel 3.18 describes God's transformation of nature:

> On that day
> the mountains shall drip sweet wine,
>   the hills shall flow with milk,
> and all the stream beds of Judah
>   shall flow with water;
> a fountain shall come forth from the house of the LORD
>   and water the Wadi Shittim.

Have you considered?
APOCALYPTIC AND THE RESURRECTION OF THE DEAD

Given the widespread presence of the belief in the resurrection of the dead found in the New Testament, some people may be surprised to find relatively few references to this idea in the Old Testament. In its place, the dominant perspective remains that the deceased descend to Sheol, a shadowy, dusty, gloomy underworld (Ps. 88.6; Job 10.20–22), where they experience a weakened semi-existence (Isa.14.9–10), largely devoid of God's presence (Ps. 88.4–5; Isa. 38.18–19). The apocalyptic authors, however, witness to a growing realization that God has more in plan – that fellowship with God cannot be broken by death and that God's justice must be established, whether in this life or the next. Thus, a belief in the resurrection of the dead is a key element in the future expectation of many of the apocalyptic writings.

Probably the earliest reference to the concept of personal, as opposed to national,* resurrection is found in Isaiah 26.19, part of the so-called Isaiah Apocalypse (for more details see below):

> Your dead shall live, their corpses shall rise.
>   O dwellers in the dust, awake and sing for joy!
> For your dew is a radiant dew,
>   and the earth will give birth to those long dead.

In contrast to later texts, however, this passage does not appear to envisage a general resurrection; instead, it is a divine act which is experienced only by the faithful.

The clearest reference to the general resurrection of the dead in the Old Testament is Daniel 12.2–3:

---

* Ezekiel's well-known vision of the valley of dry bones (ch. 37) describes the revivification of the nation (which is experiencing a metaphorical death in exile) rather than the resurrection of individuals. Likewise, Hos. 6.1–2 points to the renewal/restoration of the nation following a period of divine chastisement.

Many of those who sleep in the dust of the earth shall awake, some to everlasting life, and some to shame and everlasting contempt. Those who are wise shall shine like the brightness of the sky, and those who lead many to righteousness, like the stars for ever and ever.

Here a belief in the general (but apparently not universal) resurrection of the dead is implicitly linked with divine judgement.[†] The precise fate of the two groups, however, remains unclear: terms such as 'shame' and 'everlasting contempt' are ambiguous (it is worth noting, however, that there is no indication of eternal torment), while the reference to 'shining like the stars of heaven' has been interpreted in various ways (does it envisage some form of existence akin to that of the angels; cf. Dan. 8.10?). Whichever interpretation we favour, it is clear that we have got some distance to travel before we arrive at the more fully developed Christian conception of a text such as 1 Corinthians 15.

[†] Cook has suggested that the reference to 'many' in Dan. 12.2 is an idiom referring to all God's people (private correspondence); however, most commentators argue against a universal understanding (see, for example, J. Collins, 1993: 392, Goldingay, 1989: 308).

5.2.5 Apocalyptic literature is designed to encourage its audience during times of crisis

The purpose of prophecy is manifold. It involved (but was not limited to) *prosecution* of the people for covenant faithlessness, *persuasion* to change their ways, and *prediction* of God's imminent action in judgement or salvation (Sandy, 2002: 130–1).

The purpose of apocalyptic literature, on the other hand, can be more narrowly defined: it primarily served to encourage its readers in the midst of their trials. Apocalyptic literature, like prophecy, is highly situational – it was written in order to address and respond to a specific problem in the life of the community of faith. This situation was usually one of crisis, such as rapid, destabilizing change, a severe drought or plague, or persecution.

Going deeper:
STEPHEN COOK (1962–)

It has frequently been argued that the groups responsible for composing the apocalyptic literature not only lived during a period of crisis, but also stood on the periphery of Jewish society, experiencing deprivation, alienation and oppression. According to this perspective, such groups produced apocalyptic texts because they were powerless to alter their situation themselves and their only hope was that God would intervene for them. On the basis of significant sociological research into the nature of apocalyptic or millennial groups, however, Cook has questioned this commonly held assumption. He argues that apocalyptic writings are just as likely to be produced by people who hold central positions of power within their society as they are by those on the margins, and that a number of the biblical apocalyptic texts seem to reflect the work of centrally located priests. For further details, see Cook, 1995.

For example, critical scholars often associate the book of Daniel (or at least chapters 7—12) with the crisis precipitated by the persecution of the Jews undertaken by Antiochus IV Epiphanes during the early second century BC.[7] The book can be read as a commentary on the dramatic and distressing events that occurred in Israel and the broader world during his reign, which included the desecration of the Jerusalem Temple, the outlawing of distinctive Jewish rites, and the execution of those who opposed him (for more details see box below). Daniel 7.25 appears to allude to Antiochus with its reference to the little horn 'speaking words against the Most High, wearing out the holy ones of the Most High, attempting to change the sacred seasons and the law'.

Going deeper:
WHO WAS ANTIOCHUS IV EPIPHANES AND WHAT DID HE DO?

Following the death of Alexander the Great in 323 BC, a power struggle ensued among his generals for control of his massive empire. This resulted in his realm being divided into pieces, with a dynasty known as the Seleucids gaining control over the region of Syria, which eventually incorporated Israel as well. Antiochus IV, who ruled from 175 to 164 BC, was the most infamous Seleucid ruler. Antiochus quickly got himself off-side with the Jews. He allowed the position of high priest to be bought, and plundered the Jerusalem Temple, removing everything of value, to finance his tribute payments to Rome. He also insisted on a forced policy of Hellenization which he hoped would bring greater unity to his ethnically diverse population.* This included the passing of strict laws against those religious rites and practices (such as circumcision and Sabbath observance) that marked the Jews out as a distinctive people-group. He had copies of the Torah burnt, and ordered Jews to offer unclean sacrifices to pagan gods. Those who opposed

---

* 'Hellenization' refers to the attempt to spread Greek culture (and language), often through combining Greek culture with local, indigenous practices or elements.

---

[7] Conservative scholars have tended to argue for an earlier date for the entire book (late sixth or early fifth century), suggesting that it was composed shortly after the events it narrates. For further details see Chapter 2. There is a broad consensus among critical and conservative scholars alike that chapters 7—12 are primarily concerned with developments which took place during the reign of Antiochus.

Antiochus were dealt with in a ruthless fashion. The conflict between Antiochus and the Jews reached a climax on 25 December 167 BC when he desecrated the Jerusalem Temple by setting up an altar to Zeus and offering a pig as a sacrifice. This act is alluded to in the book of Daniel as 'the abomination that makes desolate' (11.31). Antiochus had gone too far and his actions would have serious consequences: the ensuing Jewish uprising would lead to the Maccabean Revolt.

Apocalyptic seeks to encourage, comfort and exhort the community to continued faithfulness, in spite of whatever opposition or problems its members may be facing. It affirms that such crises are only temporary – God remains in control and he will soon act to judge the wicked and vindicate the righteous.

Going deeper:
SPEECH-ACT THEORY AND THE INTERPRETATION OF APOCALYPTIC TEXTS

Speech-act theory attempts to explain how speakers use language not only to convey information but also to accomplish intended actions and evoke certain responses. In short, speech-act theorists suggest that texts not only *say* things; they *do* things.

Although they may be defined slightly differently, speech-act theorists commonly argue that utterances have three levels or dimensions:

1 'locution' refers to what is said – utterances have *meaning*;
2 'illocution' refers to what we intend to accomplish in what we say – utterances have *force*;
3 'perlocution' refers to what speakers do to hearers by saying something, i.e. the actual responses speakers evoke from their hearers – utterances have *consequences* or results.

For example, 'It's hot in here' is a statement about the perceived high temperature of the room in which the speaker is located. This is said with a certain force: it could be an indirect *request* for someone to open the window, or it could be a *complaint* implying that someone should know better than to keep the windows closed. And this statement might have an effect – it could result in someone opening the windows to cool the room down.*

From a pragmatic perspective, speech-act theory has been important for biblical interpretation primarily in terms of drawing attention to what the biblical authors were trying to achieve through their writing. In terms of the apocalyptic literature, this might involve:

---

* <http://instructional1.calstatela.edu/lkamhis/tesl565_sp04/troy/spchact.htm>, accessed 20 November 2013.

1 providing comfort and hope in the face of opposition;
2 raising people's hope of God's protection and deliverance;
3 strengthening resolve and a call to continued faithfulness and commitment.

When it comes to the interpretation of apocalyptic texts, therefore, we should not only be concerned with the question 'What is the biblical author trying to communicate?', but 'Why? What is the writer's purpose?'

This leads into a final key difference between prophecy and apocalyptic which is not explicit in Osborne's definition:

5.2.6 Apocalyptic literature is more deterministic

Human decisions and activity are important in prophecy. The fate of the nation is, to a large extent, contingent on the response of the people to the divine word given through the prophets. The prophets assert that if the people fail to hear and continue in their sinful ways, then judgement will come. If, on the other hand, they listen and repent, this may result in God changing his mind and not bringing about the judgement he had decreed (Jer. 18). Human decisions thus have the potential to shape and alter the course of history.

In apocalyptic, however, the course of history is completely predetermined by God. History is divided into precise periods of time in which kingdoms and empires will rise and fall, all brought about by the sovereign will of God. God is in complete control, overseeing what is taking place on the earth, and bringing it to his desired outcome. This divine plan cannot be hastened or thwarted by human activity.

> God may have been able, according to the preexilic and exilic prophets, to change his mind in his dealings with his people, and according to the postexilic prophets he may have become more predisposed to bless his people. But with apocalyptic, history becomes a pre-programmed drama where the actors have their parts already written for them, and they neither miss their cues nor stray from their lines. (Meier, 2009: 37)

As a result, a call for the people to change is rarely found in apocalyptic texts. In its place, the seer encourages his audience to hold on, to remain faithful, to persevere until God acts.

While identifying the characteristic features of apocalyptic is a valuable exercise, it needs to be emphasized that not all texts labelled 'apocalyptic' will share all these features, or even possess a majority of them in 'full-blown' form. This is especially the case for those texts characterized as early or proto-apocalyptic (for more details see below). The Old Testament contains a 'family' of biblical apocalyptic texts, and the intensity and nature of the family resemblance will vary from book to book (Cook, 2003: 11).

5.3 Where are apocalyptic texts found?

The most fully developed example of apocalyptic from the Old Testament is the book of Daniel, especially chapters 7—12. These chapters consist of a series of four visions, which begin with a description of the sweep of history from the time of the Babylonian Empire, through the Medes, Persians and Greeks, culminating in the arrival of Antiochus Epiphanes. These chapters affirm that although there will be conflict between nations and heavenly powers, God is ultimately in control of the world and Israel's situation, and is about to act in judgement against those who are persecuting his people. They conclude with a description of the time of the end, which will include a period of anguish 'such as has never occurred since nations first came into existence' (Dan. 12.1), as well as holding out hope for the resurrection of the dead (12.2–3), which will involve vindication for the righteous (they will experience 'everlasting life') and judgement for the wicked (they will awake to 'shame and everlasting contempt').

The presence of an apocalyptic worldview or imagination in the Old Testament, however, is not restricted to the book of Daniel. Apocalyptic elements are found in a number of prophetic texts, which are variously identified as early, proto or nascent apocalyptic.[8] Key examples include: Isaiah 24—27 (often referred to as the 'Isaiah Apocalypse'), Joel 3—4, portions of Ezekiel (especially chs 38—39), Zechariah, Isaiah 56—66 and Malachi. The preponderance of post-exilic texts suggests that apocalypticism was a relatively late development in Israel's history.

Going deeper:
WHAT IS THE PSEUDEPIGRAPHA?

The Pseudepigrapha is a collection of approximately 65 non-canonical documents which were written by Jews or Christians mainly during the period c. 250 BC–AD 200. The name 'pseudepigrapha' means 'writings with false ascriptions' and was applied to these works because the person to whom they were attributed (usually an important biblical figure or character) was not their author. The Pseudepigrapha includes approximately 19 apocalyptic documents, such as *1–3 Enoch*, the *Apocalypse of Abraham*, the *Apocalypse of Adam*, the *Apocalypse of Elijah* and the *Apocalypse of Daniel*. The most important of these is probably *1 Enoch*, for it contains the earliest examples of non-biblical apocalyptic (portions of the book pre-date the Maccabean Revolt) and is quoted in the New Testament (Jude 14–15 draws on *Enoch* 1.9).* For translations of these texts, see Charlesworth, 1983.

---
* A number of early Church Fathers, including Athenagoras, Clement of Alexandria, Irenaeus and Tertullian appear to have viewed this work as authoritative!

---
[8] Russell (1994: 31) borrows an analogy from biology to refer to these prophetic / early apocalyptic texts as 'embryonic apocalyptic'. In these texts we begin to see the basic form and appearance of the fully grown apocalyptic child which would be birthed some time around the third to second century BC.

We also have numerous examples of apocalyptic texts outside the Old Testament canon. Apocalypticism was very common in the biblical world from near the end of the Old Testament period through to the second century AD: Jewish, Christian, Graeco-Roman and Persian examples have been preserved.[9] Key documents include *4 Ezra*, which is found in the Apocrypha, as well as several works from the Pseudepigrapha, such as *1 Enoch* and *2 Baruch*. These texts have the potential to shed much light on their canonical biblical counterparts. For example, they help us get into the mindset and worldview of the apocalyptic authors (a perspective which is very different from that of people who live in the modern West), and thus provide us with an intellectual context for understanding the message of apocalyptic passages from Daniel and the Old Testament prophets.

5.4 Guidelines for interpreting apocalyptic texts

Apocalyptic texts present unique challenges to the modern interpreter. 'No other genre of the Bible has been so fervently read with such depressing results' (Tate, 2008: 173). Our problems are largely a result of the fact that the apocalyptic genre has no real modern equivalent.

Most biblical genres have a similar modern counterpart. For example, modern proverbs such as 'A stitch in time saves nine' or 'Too many cooks spoil the broth' resemble the kind of wisdom we find in the book of Proverbs. This means that when we encounter examples of these genres in the biblical text we are already familiar, to a certain extent, with the basic rules of the interpretive game. We know, for example, that proverbs are not always true (sometimes it is helpful to have a lot of help in the kitchen), and that context may determine whether or not a particular proverb is applicable (it often depends on the size of the kitchen!). Unfortunately, however, there is no real modern equivalent to the apocalyptic genre, and thus twenty-first-century readers are stuck when it comes to understanding the rules of this interpretive game.

The following guidelines should help you better understand these sometimes weird and wonderful texts:

5.4.1 Focus on the big picture

Impressionistic art can serve as a helpful analogy for orienting our reading of apocalyptic texts (Sandy, 2002: 127–8). An impressionistic painting is best appreciated from a distance. These works are composed of fine lines, dabs of paint and brush strokes that 'combine to depict scenes of unusual vividness and emotion' (Sandy, 2002: 127). If we stand too close, however, if we concentrate

---

[9] For a fuller discussion of the non-biblical apocalyptic writings see J. Collins, *Apocalypse: The Morphology of a Genre*, Semeia 14. SBL: Missoula, 1979; F. Murphy, *Apocalypticism in the Bible and Its World: A Comprehensive Introduction*, Grand Rapids: Baker, 2012.

Figure 5.3 An example of impressionistic art: *Haystacks (Effects of Snow and Sun)* **by Claude Monet (1890–1)**

Taken from a photograph by Szilas / Wikimedia Commons.

simply on the lines and dabs themselves, we are unlikely to grasp what the artist intended to convey – all we will end up seeing are lines, dabs and strokes which look rather peculiar and random in their placement. Instead, we need to take a step back and consider the work in its entirety. When we do this, we are able to appreciate how those apparently random and disjointed paint strokes, dabs and lines in fact end up working together to produce a coherent and striking whole (see Fig. 5.3).

Likewise, apocalyptic texts need to be appreciated from a distance. When reading apocalyptic texts it is worth stepping back and trying to grasp the point of the vision as a whole. What is the overall effect? What is the big picture? What is the overarching sweep of the vision or narrative? Ultimately, we need to move beyond the details to determine the primary message(s) of the entire vision. The ever-present risk is that modern readers will get so bogged down in the details of the visions that they fail to grasp the bigger picture. Or, to draw another analogy, they will see the trees but miss the forest. Individual details may be important (after all, the only reason we have a bigger picture is because it is made up of smaller details), or they may not. What is *always* important, however, is the significance of the vision as a whole. And, of course, it is often when we have grasped the big picture that the details within this make more sense.

Once we have grasped the big picture of the vision, it is time to focus on the details. The further we move from the general (the 'big picture') to the specific (the 'details'), the less certain our interpretations may become (Sandy, 2002: 124):

In other words, while we may be confident that we have grasped the meaning of the vision as a whole, the significance of certain specific elements within this may elude us.

> This is not unexpected, given the allusive nature of apocalyptic visions. For much of the vision is an earthly way to think about a heavenly reality, or a present way to think about a future reality. So given our earthly and present limitations, we cannot expect to understand the meaning of each detail.
>
> (Sandy, 2002: 124)

Key issues we may wish to consider when analysing details include:

1 the significance of the detail in its original historical-cultural context (see below) and whether the detail is symbolic in some way – does it represent a 'deeper' reality?
2 whether the detail is primarily predictive of subsequent events or points to past or present realities;
3 whether the detail is simply included for the sake of effect, colour or impact.

Details may not possess a symbolic dimension due to the fact that apocalyptic texts are more like parables than allegories. Parables and allegories are similar in that both usually contain a secondary, deeper level of meaning. For example, in Jesus' famous parable of the prodigal son (Luke 15), the father represents God, the prodigal son represents the tax collectors and sinners, while the older brother represents the Pharisees and scribes (15.1). A key difference between parables and allegories, however, is the level of representation. In the case of parables not every element possesses a deeper dimension. For example, it is unlikely that Jesus intended the robe, ring and sandals that the father gives to the younger son upon his return (v. 22) to represent anything other than his ongoing love for his son, his joy to see him return, and his desire to welcome him back into the family.[10] These details simply add colour and life to the story.

---

[10] This is contrary to much traditional interpretation of the parable. For example, Clement of Alexandria (c. AD 150–215) suggested that the robe is the robe of immortality, the ring is the seal of the Trinity, and the sandals are shoes which do not wear out and are suited for the journey to heaven.

In a similar vein, we should not expect every single detail of an apocalyptic vision to have a secondary level of meaning. While this may be the case for some elements (e.g. the four rams of Dan. 7 represent four world empires), other details may be included simply for dramatic effect or emotive power. For example, the goat's defeat of the ram in Daniel 8 is described in copious and colourful detail: the goat charges at the ram in great rage, it attacks the ram furiously, it strikes the ram, it shatters the ram's two horns, it knocks the ram to the ground, it tramples on the ram. It is unlikely, however, that each of these descriptions of the goat's activity has its own unique significance (e.g. the goat's striking the ram does not essentially refer to something different from its trampling on the ram); they are just different ways to powerfully visualize the same event (Sandy, 2002: 117–18).

It should be recognized, however, that the 'plan of attack' which I have outlined above – from big picture to details – does not need to be followed in a strictly or rigidly linear fashion. Our interpretation of the big picture of an apocalyptic vision will shape our understanding of its details, but our interpretation of the details will also shape our understanding of the big picture. A hermeneutical circle is at work. Nevertheless, I would suggest that our starting point should be at the macro, rather than micro, level as this provides the necessary context within which the details must be understood.

5.4.2 Interpret images within their original historical context

As suggested above, a key feature of the apocalyptic genre is its use of dramatic imagery. For example, in the book of Daniel we encounter strange beasts rising out of the sea (chs 7; 8), and the resurrected dead shining like the stars of heaven (ch. 12). In Zechariah we read of golden lampstands (ch. 4), flying scrolls and a woman in a basket named 'Wickedness' (ch. 5). Modern interpreters are often confused by the bizarre imagery and symbolism of these books, and as a result are tempted to interpret the imagery in the light of current cultural meaning or possibilities.

Have you considered?
APOCALYPTIC SYMBOLISM AND MODERN POLITICAL CARTOONS

It is commonly suggested that the imagery we find in apocalyptic texts, especially the book of Revelation, is similar to modern political cartoons. In these cartoons, well-known images are used to represent entities or nations. For example, the bulldog symbolizes Britain, the bear Russia, and the bald eagle the USA (see Fig. 5.4). The use of such imagery in political cartoons is based on the assumption that the reader is aware of the meaning of these images, and if the interpreter lacks this knowledge, he or she will struggle to make sense of what the author or artist wished to convey.

Figure 5.4 An example of a political cartoon: 'The real trouble will come with the "wake"' by Joseph Keppler. Note the animals used to represent Russia, Britain, Germany, Austria, Italy, France and Japan fighting over the body of China (a dragon). The USA (an eagle) looks on

From *Puck* (15 August 1900) / Wikimedia Commons.

While it may seem quite strange to us, the kind of apocalyptic symbolism or imagery we find in these books was actually quite common within its original historical context. We can assume that the original recipients of these texts would have been able to figure out the meaning and significance of the images. After all, the purpose of apocalyptic documents is to 'reveal' or 'unveil' God's plans, not make them incomprehensible.

So how do we go about interpreting such imagery? Our first port of call should be other biblical and apocalyptic texts from the time. Since many of these images are reasonably conventional, their use in other texts may well shed light on their meaning and significance in the specific passage under consideration. For example, the image of a dragon is regularly used to portray the powers who oppose the Lord or his people, including hostile foreign kings (Isa. 27.1; 51.9; Ezek. 29.3; 32.2; Rev. 12).

Have you considered?
THE SOURCES OF APOCALYPTIC LANGUAGE AND IMAGERY

The language and imagery we find in apocalyptic texts has a rich and varied background. The two key influences are scriptural (especially prophetic) themes and images, and ancient Near Eastern (or in the case of Revelation, Graeco-Roman) mythological ideas and elements.

1 *Earlier scriptural themes and images.* The 'end times' revelations of the apocalyptic seers are, in fact, often expressed using traditional language and
symbols drawn from Israel's religious heritage. 'Echoes and allusions to earlier
Scriptures form the fabric of their [i.e. the apocalyptic authors'] imagination'
(Cook, 2003: 64).

For example, in Zechariah 3.8 the prophet refers to a figure called the 'Branch',
using an expression for the messianic king already found in Jeremiah 23.5,
while Isaiah 63.1–6 makes significant use of Divine Warrior traditions (especially the idea that Yahweh personally engages in conflict against his and his
people's foes), earlier chapters from the book of Isaiah (esp. 41; 44; 45; 51),
and the book of Psalms (esp. Pss. 24.7–10; 44.3; 60.3; 75.8; 98.1) (Cook, 2003:
114–15). Sometimes earlier scriptural texts are explicitly cited, with the apocalyptic authors commenting on and interpreting this material. For example, Ezekiel
38.17 identifies Gog of Magog as the one 'of whom I spoke in former days by
my servants the prophets of Israel, who in those days prophesied for years
that I would bring you against them', while Daniel 9 provides an interpretation
of Jeremiah 25.11–12; 29.10, suggesting that Israel's exile will not last for
70 years but 70 weeks of years (i.e. 490 years).

2 *Mythological ideas and elements.* The apocalyptic authors occasionally draw
on mythological material from the broader ancient Near Eastern world. Such
myths provided the authors with a ready-made source of language and motifs
to describe the transcendent and 'supermundane' realities they wished to speak
about. The so-called Isaiah Apocalypse (Isa. 24—27) contains two noticeable
examples. In 25.6–10 the prophet describes the Lord's great act of salvation,
which includes God destroying 'the shroud that is cast over all peoples, the sheet
that is spread over all nations; he will swallow up death for ever' (vv. 7–8a). The
description of God 'swallowing up' death is particularly interesting. It is likely that
this image has been deliberately chosen as it involves the reversal of a Canaanite
mythological motif which saw the god of death, Mot, 'swallow up' gods and
human beings.* Death will thus experience itself what it has been doing to
others for so long – it will be swallowed up once and for all.

The second example is found in Isaiah 27.1. Here the prophet announces
that the Lord 'with his cruel and great and strong sword will punish Leviathan
the fleeing serpent, Leviathan the twisting serpent, and he will kill the dragon
that is in the sea'. This victory of the supreme God over the forces of chaos,
embodied in the form of a great serpent or dragon from the sea, is a common
motif in ancient Near Eastern literature (for further details, see Chapter 3).
The key difference in Isaiah's usage, however, is that the victory is eschat-
ologized: instead of being a past event (God's defeat of the serpent is usually

---

* For example, one text from Ugarit describes how Mot 'extends a lip to the earth, a lip to the heavens, he
extends a tongue to the stars. Baal must enter his belly, down into his mouth he must go' (*KTU* 1.5 ii 2–5;
cf. 1.5 ii 7–8, translation from Wyatt, 1998: 120). 'The main characteristic of Mot is that he is a voracious
consumer of gods and men. He has an enormous mouth and an appetite to match' (Healey, 1999: 599).

associated with the creation of the heavens and earth (cf. Ps. 74.13–17)), here it refers to God's future, ultimate defeat of the forces of evil which oppose him (see Fig. 5.5).

Sometimes both earlier prophetic writings and ancient Near Eastern myth seem to be in play in a single text. For example, Daniel 4.10–18 records Nebuchadnezzar's second dream in which a great tree 'at the centre of the earth' represents the king's own greatness and might. This image of a tree at the *axis mundi* was widely used in ancient Near Eastern mythology, where it was employed as a symbol of Creation and world order. At the same time, the similarities between this passage and Ezekiel 31.1–9 (even though the oracle is directed against Egypt) 'are too close not to imply influence' (Hewitt, 1977: 106), suggesting that the author has been impacted by both ancient Near Eastern and Israelite streams of tradition.

Figure 5.5 'The destruction of Leviathan (Isa. 27)' from Doré's *English Bible*

Engraving from G. Doré, *The Holy Bible, with Illustrations by Gustave Doré*. London and New York: Cassell, Petter and Galpin, 1866–70. Wikimedia Commons.

At the same time, however, we should not simply assume that the meaning of an image will be exactly the same as its usage elsewhere. Images can be transformed and shaped by the desires of the author; it is not uncommon for traditional images and symbols to undergo an 'apocalyptic shift in orientation' (Cook, 2003: 36). This can be seen, for example, in the discussion of Isaiah 27.1 above. The interpreter should therefore ensure that he or she focuses on the meaning of the image within its specific context.

Because we come from a vastly different chronological and cultural context from the author and original audience, we will often need the advice of a trusted and dependable guide when confronted by apocalyptic imagery. Without such help we run the risk of importing our own ideas into the text. Fortunately, there are a number of good resources available: most detailed commentaries will include extended treatments of the key images of a passage, and there are a number of books which specifically focus on the use of imagery in the Bible. A good example of the latter is L. Ryken, J. Wilhoit and T. Longman III, 1998.

Instead of providing the definitive 'answers' we perhaps might like, these resources will sometimes propose multiple (even contradictory) interpretations of a single image. For example, the fourth beast of Daniel 7 has been variously interpreted as the Greek Empire, the Roman Empire, the Arabs, Christendom (by Jewish interpreters) and the papacy (by Protestants)! It is therefore incumbent on the individual interpreter to decide which interpretation he or she thinks is the most likely. Literary context may be helpful in this regard as individual visions are usually part of larger sequences of visions. Thus, the meaning of one vision may clarify or shed light on another: 'No vision or detail functions by itself' (Osborne, 2006: 286). It needs to be acknowledged, however, that an author may use a single image in multiple ways, and thus literary context is not an automatic, fail-safe guide. For example, the woman in Revelation 12 is clearly a positive figure, while the woman in chapter 17 is evil, and it would be a serious mistake to equate the two.

5.4.3 Focus on paradigms

Our concern to interpret apocalyptic texts in the light of their original historical context should not lead us to think that biblical interpretation simply involves 'cracking their code' – identifying the specific historical realities to which they were referring. If we only focus on apocalyptic texts as coded descriptions of the *past* (or, for that matter, coded previews of events to unfold in the *future*), we may end up depriving the texts of any power to speak their words of encouragement and hope into the *present*.

Historical references and second-century BC events do not exhaust the meaning or insights of a book such as Daniel. The monstrous beasts of Daniel 7 and 8 do not only signify empires that have already come and gone. If this were the case, the contemporary reader would find little of value here – 'in the twenty first century, Daniel's monsters would be of taxidermic interest only' (Cook, 2003: 141). Rather than being restricted to a specific geographical and chronological context, Daniel's images and imagination, its expansive and awesome visions, 'burst the bounds of its original historical milieu' (Cook, 2003: 142). These texts 'resonate with truth on multiple occasions' and thus have a 'rich capacity to speak to multiple situations over a long expanse of time' as seen in the way the text has continued to speak to the community of faith throughout its history (Cook, 2003: 51, 52). Hence, while texts such as Daniel 7.9–14; 11.40—12.4 are, on one level, references to Antiochus IV Epiphanes, on another they are 'open ended narratives about God's certain triumph over tyranny' which serve as a source of encouragement to people living in the midst of crisis, no matter their time or place (Towner, 1987: 281).

One way in which we can seek to hear the contemporary resonances of these texts is by considering what is paradigmatic within them. In the apocalyptic literature 'we have no timetables, no histories written in advance; instead, we have paradigms, models, types that can make our present experience meaningful and shape our attitude toward our own future' (Towner, 1987: 281). For example, we may wish to consider what the text reveals about:

1 the nature and workings of evil and those who oppose God and his people;
2 the attitude of God's people to suffering, troubles and persecution;
3 the response of God both to his faithful people and to those who oppose his will;
4 God's ultimate victory over evil and injustice, and its implications for life in the present.

Such reflective activity will require us to engage theologically with the text. This is a valuable exercise as it serves the ultimate purpose of the text: 'the writer wanted to turn the reader toward God, not just toward future events' (Osborne, 2006: 287).

Going deeper:
DAVID RUSSELL ON THE PARADIGMATIC NATURE OF APOCALYPTIC TEXTS

Generally speaking, such predictions are rightly to be understood in dynamic rather than in static terms, providing a paradigm for God's action in all succeeding generations. That is, the future reference has to do, not with forecasting specifically detailed events in some far distant time, but with the working out of the divine purpose in every generation; not with a predetermined plan proceeding inexorably according to some unalterable program, but a divine principle showing God at work fulfilling his divine will; not a precisely worked-out timetable of future events, but a pledge of God's presence and help, not least in times of trial.   (Russell, 1994: 105–6)

5.5 Potential problems to avoid

The main pitfall we should seek to avoid when interpreting the apocalyptic literature is assuming that the apocalyptic visions primarily refer to contemporary realities. People who utilize this approach typically spend all their time attempting to correlate the biblical text with events and developments in their own day. While it is important to affirm that these books do address the issues of twenty-first-century Christians (just as they have addressed the concerns of Christians throughout history), adopting such a stance towards the apocalyptic texts is deeply problematic, as I will explain in the discussion of preaching from the prophets (see 6.7.1 below).

Going deeper:
HAL LINDSAY AND THE INTERPRETATION OF APOCALYPTIC TEXTS

Perhaps the best-known modern attempt to link apocalyptic texts directly with contemporary developments and realities is the work of Hal Lindsay, and in particular, his best-sellers, *The Late Great Planet Earth* and *There's a New World Coming.** Lindsay suggests, for example, that the fiery judgement of God envisaged in Ezekiel 38—39 is a description of nuclear war (Lindsay and Carlson, 1970: 150–1), while the locusts which appear as agents of God's wrath in Revelation 9 may be Cobra helicopters; their deadly sting is the nerve-gas sprayed from the helicopters' tails (Lindsay, 1984: 126).

---

* H. Lindsay and C. Carlson, *The Late Great Planet Earth*, Grand Rapids: Zondervan, 1970; H. Lindsay, *There's a New World Coming: An In-Depth Analysis of the Book of Revelation*, Eugene: Harvest, 1984.

5.5.1 Historicizing

This approach to the text sits at the other end of the spectrum from attempts to identify contemporary fulfilments. Instead of seeking to pinpoint supposed correlations between the apocalyptic texts and twenty-first-century events, proponents of this approach 'preoccupy themselves with merely historical questions about the accuracy or otherwise of its [i.e. Daniel's] presentation of sixth- and second-century history, as if the solving of such questions constituted the interpretation of the book' (Goldingay, 1989: ix).

While such an approach correctly assumes that these texts need to be understood in the light of their original historical context, it fails to appreciate that the message of such texts transcends their original historical context. They continue to speak a word which challenges the powerful and comforts the oppressed, no matter where and when they live.

5.5.2 Decontextualizing

This mistake involves failing to appreciate the message of the apocalyptic literature in the light of the teachings of the rest of Scripture. Apocalyptic is but one element of the total biblical revelation, and it needs to be heard in the context of the claims of the Bible as a whole.

Going deeper:
MÜNTZER AND APOCALYPTIC

One of the most famous examples of apocalyptic texts fuelling radical, violent action is Thomas Müntzer. Müntzer was an early Reformation-era German theologian. In 1524 he preached a sermon based on Daniel 2 before one of the Saxon princes, Duke John, entitled 'Sermon to the Princes' (*Die Fürstenpredigt*). He argued in this that the last of the world empires was coming to an end, that the arrival of the kingdom of God was imminent, and that the princes should take up the sword to slay God's enemies. Within a year Müntzer had taken up arms himself as part of the Peasants' Revolt, leading a group of about 8,000 peasants at the battle of Frankenhausen (15 May 1525) who were convinced that God would intervene on their side. Müntzer and his forces, however, were quickly defeated, and Müntzer himself was imprisoned, tortured and subsequently decapitated.

The history of the interpretation of apocalyptic literature shows that decontextualizing often leads to two extremes. The first is the use of these texts to advocate a virtual withdrawal from social and political involvement in anticipation of God's imminent intervention in history. This line of thinking assumes that there is little need for the community of faith to concern itself with issues such as world peace or social justice in the present because God is about to destroy the world and most of its inhabitants, and snatch the chosen few to heaven. The second tendency is to appropriate apocalyptic texts as the basis for extreme, militant action against other nations or religions, with proponents of this approach often seeing themselves as the means by which God will bring about his eagerly anticipated kingdom on earth. Both extremes, quietist passivity and violent activism, however, stand in sharp tension with the broader teaching of the Old and New Testaments. It is difficult to reconcile both, for example, with Jesus' blessing on the peacemakers (Matt. 5.9) and the implicit call to make peace which this entails (it is the peacemakers who are called children of God!).

5.6 Summary

The unique content and style of the apocalyptic literature of the Old Testament presents numerous challenges to contemporary interpreters. Such challenges, however, are nothing new – Daniel himself was baffled and bewildered by his visions, at least one of which he found 'beyond understanding' (Dan. 8.27 NIV). When we read a passage like this we may be tempted to throw our hands in the air – after all, if the original recipient of these cryptic visions struggled with their meaning, what hope do we have? There are, however, a number of things that we can put in place to guide our reading: we should focus on the big picture, interpret images within their original historical context, and focus on the paradigms the text embodies. Still, it is important to recognize that reading apocalyptic is often a sustained lesson in humility – certainty regularly eludes us, and our curiosity is seldom sated.[11]

> But there remains a sense in which apocalyptic is mysterious. What all this means is not completely clear. To remove that quality is to change the atmosphere of the genre that makes it what it is. 'We do not make contact with the prophet's mind by reducing each figure in his narrative to some empirical equivalent.' To read the Apocalypse with a microscope, ever striving to decipher the significance of the most minute detail, defrauds the genre of its intended function. To hear apocalyptic, to feel its emotive language, to sense its mystery is to hear it aright.
>
> (Sandy, 2002: 127, citing Paul Minear)

Although the apocalyptic literature claims to unveil the future, the books' focus on the transcendent, their use of symbolism and the presence of historical ambiguity means that it is an enigmatic unveiling at best.

Further reading

Cook, S. *The Apocalyptic Literature*, IBT. Nashville: Abingdon, 2003.

Murphy, F. *Apocalypticism in the Bible and Its World: A Comprehensive Introduction*. Grand Rapids: Baker, 2012.

Russell, D. S. *Prophecy and the Apocalyptic Dream: Protest and Promise*. Peabody: Hendrickson, 1994.

Sandy, D. Brent. *Plowshares and Pruning Hooks: Rethinking the Language of Biblical Prophecy and Apocalyptic*. Downers Grove: IVP, 2002.

Towner, W. 'The Preacher in the Lions' Den', in Mays, J. and P. Achtemeier (eds), *Interpreting the Prophets*. Philadelphia: Fortress, 1987, pp. 273–84.

---

[11] Duvall and Hays make the important point that 'People who must satisfy their curiosity or people who are unwilling to live with any uncertainty are those most likely to read into Revelation things that are not there' (2012: 317).

6

Guidelines for preaching
from the prophets

6.1 Introduction

The basis for the majority of the prophetic books is oral proclamation.[1]
The prophets repeatedly *spoke* into the life of the people of God on the basis
of the divine word which had been revealed to them. Therefore, it seems
worthwhile to conclude our discussion of interpreting the prophets with
some consideration of how these texts might function as a resource for
Christian proclamation today.

So far in this book we have focused on understanding the prophetic message
in terms of the 'there and then' (i.e. understanding what the prophets were
saying to their original audience, the Israelites, during the first millennium BC).
This is essential; however, it would be a mistake to assume that as a result of
this process we are automatically able to proclaim their message to the 'here
and now' (i.e. to our contemporary audience).

> Careful explanation of the text can elucidate the historical background,
> explain key words, and identify literary strategies or power struggles. It can even
> show why the text used to matter. Such explanation does not automatically
> show why the text still matters now or even that it should matter.
>
> (Farris, 2008: 180–1)

In what follows, therefore, I will lay out some guidelines for preaching from
the prophets, for bridging the 'chasm' between the world of ancient Israel
and the contemporary world. Rather than providing an overview of the
general process of moving from text to sermon (such surveys can easily be
found in other resources; see, for example, the works of Duvall and Hays
and Robinson in the 'Further reading' section below), I will focus on considerations which are particularly pertinent for preaching from the prophets.
The unique nature of this genre means that there are some distinct issues
and challenges that we need to be aware of.

Before we go too far, however, a preliminary word of realism is in order – we
need to recognize that preaching from the prophets may be a time-consuming
process. It is likely that you will need more time (at least initially) to prepare
a sermon based on the prophets than a text from the Gospels or Epistles. There

---

[1] For further details, see Chapter 1.

are a number of reasons for this, not the least of which is that we often don't bring the same level of pre-understanding to the prophetic texts: we are not as familiar with their world or their basic message as we are for much of the New Testament.[2] It is therefore essential that preachers set aside ample preparation time; inadequate preparation may result in a lack of confidence when it comes to the act of preaching and a lack of clarity in the sermon itself. While the 'lead-in' time for each preacher will vary, someone with little knowledge or experience of preaching from the prophets may want to begin preparatory study a couple of months before he or she actually plans to preach.

6.2 Choose preaching texts carefully

When it comes to text selection, some expositors advocate a careful verse-by-verse working through of the entire prophetic book. In my opinion, however, this is not required, nor is it necessarily wise (unless perhaps you are dealing with one of the smaller books). As suggested in Chapter 1, the prophetic books are essentially anthologies; they are the prophets' 'greatest hits'. Hence, we tend to find each prophet primarily focusing on a few key themes which he revisits over and over again. For example, the book of Hosea possesses three central themes: the love and commitment of the Lord for his people, the faithlessness (and imminent judgement) of Israel in its religious and political life, and the eventual restoration of Israel after judgement. These themes are developed in different ways and approached from different perspectives throughout the book, but essentially they represent the heart of what the prophet has to say.

An approach which seeks to work through the text in an all-inclusive fashion, therefore, is likely to be somewhat repetitive. The preacher who chooses to do an exhaustive sermon series on Hosea may well find that he or she is saying the same basic things over and over again. In my opinion, a better approach is to focus on a select number of key passages, which provide a suitable introduction to and overview of the prophet's message for the congregation. A handy resource in this context is Achtemeier, 1998a. Achtemeier discusses each of the minor prophets, briefly explaining the historical and theological context for each book, before identifying a number of key texts and sermon possibilities. For example, from the book of Hosea she identifies four key passages: 1.1–8; 2.14–23; 6.1–6; 11.1–11. Alternatively, the relevant articles in a number of Bible dictionaries might highlight the key portions of the book. This more focused approach ensures variety, while introducing the audience to the heart of each prophet's message. In a six-month period it would be possible to work through the three major prophets or a significant

---

[2] Of course, this lack of pre-understanding may be a good thing, for our pre-understanding can sometimes hinder our exegesis of the biblical text.

number of the minor prophets.[3] This approach provides the members of the congregation with a basic framework for understanding the prophet's message themselves and a context for their own reading of the biblical text rather than 'spoon-feeding' them everything they need to know.

The need to select texts for proclamation may be obviated by the use of a lectionary. These are generally helpful as they encourage the preacher to cover a greater breadth of Scripture than his or her personal preferences might otherwise allow, and provide a coherent sequence for sermons connected with the Christian year. At the same time, however, the lack of attention devoted to the prophets in some lectionaries is potentially problematic. For example, Achtemeier (1989: 126) has analysed the citation of prophetic texts in the three-year ecumenical lectionary and arrived at the following figures:

Isaiah	53
Jeremiah	19
Ezekiel	9
Daniel	3
Hosea	4
Joel	2
Amos	6
Jonah	2
Micah	2
Habakkuk	1
Zephaniah	4
Zechariah	2
Malachi	3

In short, most of the prophets apart from Isaiah receive minimal 'air time', and some, including Obadiah, Nahum and Haggai, are not included at all! 'The result has been an incomplete presentation of the canonical revelation and a neglect of exceedingly fruitful preaching materials' (Achtemeier, 1989: 126).[4] Hence, I would argue that an ability to identify appropriate texts for proclamation is essential for all students of the prophetic literature whether they come from traditions which favour a lectionary or not.

6.3 Identify appropriate analogies

Preaching the prophets well requires an ability to identify appropriate analogies. Analogies are similar to metaphors and similes in that they involve the

---

[3] The alternative is to spend a significant amount of time working through a single book. For example, Block proposes that 'Unless congregations already have great confidence in their pastors, no series on Ezekiel should last longer than twenty-five or thirty weeks' (2010: 171). Such an approach, however, is not well suited to the Australian cultural context (nor I suggest most of the Western world) where audiences are accustomed to greater variety.

[4] Achtemeier also suggests that the Common Lectionary 'has not remedied this situation' (1989: 126).

comparison of two different things which are alike in some way. 'Analogy is not identification but the perception of similarity. Our situation is not the same as that of the first readers or hearers of a text. It may be similar, however' (Farris, 2008: 180).

Identifying analogies essentially involves asking the question: 'To what shall we compare this (person, place, thing or event) in our lives and the lives of our listeners?' (Williams, 2008: 183).[5] For example, it has frequently been suggested that the situation of Israel during the Babylonian exile is analogous to the situation of the Church today; in both instances we are dealing with a once-great power whose influence has waned and whose symbols of meaning are mocked and dismissed. Because analogies involve finding points of connection between the world of the text and the world of the listeners, they engage the congregation and help them enter into the experience of the text with greater freshness and immediacy. Good analogies help the text come alive.

Have you considered?
PROBLEMS WITH ANALOGIES

It is sometimes difficult to identify appropriate analogies: there may be no equivalent modern parallel to a textual element, or possible parallels shed little additional light on the text itself. If this is the case the preacher could take the time to spell out why there are no suitable parallels in the modern world rather than creating a forced analogy. Such an explanation will leave the audience with a better understanding of the unique realities and dynamics which are present in the biblical text and the reasons for these.

Some analogies are better than others (just as some similes and metaphors are better than others). In their desire to be relevant, it is common for preachers to set up a simple equation: the prophets condemned injustices they saw in the world around them; we too are called to condemn similar injustices in our world today. In fact, this is often what is meant by the label 'prophetic preaching': preaching that is focused on critiquing modern social structures and injustices and exhorting believers to social action.

Such an emphasis *may* be appropriate at times. This *may* be a faithful proclamation of the text. I would argue, however, that in most instances such an approach is based on an imperfect analogy. The primary audience of the prophets was the covenant people of God, either the northern kingdom of

---

[5] Williams goes on to suggest, 'The general question when beginning to look for contemporary analogies for an ancient text is, When have my listeners experienced something analogous to the events of the text?' (2008: 183).

Israel or the southern kingdom of Judah, and not the nations around them.[6] This means that the primary target for the prophetic message today should not be those outside but those within the Church, the new-covenant people of God, the 'Israel of God' (Gal. 6.16).[7] Preachers need to consider how the people of God themselves may be perpetrating abusive practices and attitudes and what changes may thus need to be made (cf. Matt. 7.1–5), rather than spending all our time and energy condemning those outside the Church (an approach which may leave those within its walls feeling comfortable and possibly even smug). The prophetic ministry involves calling the people of God to be a community with God at its centre, a community which embodies an alternative vision of what it means to be a human society:

> But in the absence of our embodying such an alternative vision, the attempt to exercise a prophetic ministry by the use of prophetic words is surely unlikely to have much effect. It is we ourselves who need to heed the prophetic word so that we may become the alternative community. Prophets are people who call the church to be the people of God instead of being an imitation of the world.
> (Goldingay, 2011: 318)

The prophetic preacher's focus on the people of God does not mean that he or she should not be concerned with addressing a wider audience, including the broader society, at times. The basis for doing this, however, is not the direct critique of the prophets but the recognition that the prophetic texts give voice to God's concerns: they clearly show, for example, that God calls for justice, cares for the oppressed and hates evil. To put it another way, we could say that these texts encapsulate divine priorities. (For further discussion, see the paradigmatic use of prophetic texts below.) Recognition of these divine values and priorities may well form the basis for a sermon which seeks to address the practices and policies of those both within and outside the covenant community. At the same time, however, we should recognize that such people were not the primary audience of the prophets, and thus should not be the main addressee of those who seek to speak from these texts today.

6.4 Focus on the theology of the text

When we preach from the prophets it is sometimes easy to get bogged down in issues of morality and behaviour – telling people what they need to do or what they should avoid. There are two key problems with this emphasis. First, it can lack genuine transformative power. The issue for the majority of

---

[6] This is true even for the so-called 'oracles against the nations'. Although these are *addressed* to foreign nations, it is unlikely that they were actually delivered there; their *audience* was the people of God. Likewise, while the prophet Jonah addresses a foreign nation, the book itself was written for the covenant people.

[7] Of course, this is not to equate the Church with Israel, or to suggest that they are one and the same thing. Like similes and metaphors, analogies involve the comparison of two *distinct* things. Therefore, in our preaching we need to be cognizant of the ways in which the New Testament Church is both similar to and different from Old Testament Israel, in both its nature and its calling.

the people in our congregations is not lack of knowledge – they usually know what they should and should not be doing. What they do need, however, is a renewed vision of why such actions are important; they require, in the words of Brueggemann, 'transformed imaginations':

> We now know (or think we know) that human transformation (the way people change) does not happen through didacticism or through excessive certitude but through the playful entertainment of another scripting of reality that may subvert the old given text and its interpretation and lead to the embrace of an alternative text and its redescription of reality.   (Brueggemann, 2005: 20)

Hence, a heavily didactic, morality-focused approach which is not accompanied by a renewed vision of God and reality is somewhat naïve in that it is unlikely to bring about the change for which it calls.

Going deeper:
ACHTEMEIER ON GREAT PREACHING

Elizabeth Achtemeier was an outstanding preacher, lecturer and scholar who served as the professor of Bible and homiletics at Union Theological Seminary in Virginia. When asked to identify the characteristics that separate great preaching from mediocre preaching, she responded:

> the principle (*sic*) thing that should be said is that great preachers talk mostly about God and not about human problems. It is very easy for anybody to tell what is wrong with our world and what are the common struggles and sins of us human beings. We have only to look about us or to read the morning headlines. Even a twelve year old can compile a list of the evils in our society. But it takes a great preacher to say what God is doing about them.   (1998b: 1)

The second problem with this emphasis is that it substitutes what is secondary and contingent in the prophets' message (morality) for what is primary (theology).[8] The primary concern of the prophets was to announce God's word, will and acts to his people. The prophets were primarily focused on the character and activity of God – past, present and future – as it impinged on the life of the people in a given situation at a given point in time. Thus, the character and activity of God should be the central concern of those who seek to preach from these writings today.[9]

---

[8] Technically, morality cannot be separated from theology, for the latter shapes the former. My statement should not be taken to imply that the prophets were concerned with announcing timeless theological truths about God; prophetic theology is always contextual theology.

[9] This emphasis is also supported by the fact that the main point of connection between the 'then and there' of the ancient Israelites with the 'here and now' of the contemporary church audience is the faithful covenant God who is Lord of all.

In order to facilitate theological exposition of the prophets, it is worth considering a paradigmatic approach to the text. This approach is based on the assumption that the Old Testament 'contains paradigms of God's presence, purpose, and power (as well as paradigms of human response to the divine presence and purpose)' (Allen and Holbert, 1995: 32). In particular, the prophetic books provide us with recurrent pictures of divine behaviour and purpose in the world through which we may catch a glimpse of how God characteristically relates to people. We are also given insight into what God characteristically expects of people and thus may come to appreciate the priorities God has. On this basis, we can extrapolate how God may be at work in the Church and world today, and the kind of behaviour and concerns the people of God may be expected to embody in their life today. 'God's relating to people in the First Testament is not random but principled, and we learn about God's relating to us through accounts of this First Testament relating' (Goldingay, 2011: 298).

It may be helpful to compare and contrast this method with the approach that we find in a book like *The Late Great Planet Earth*,[10] which constantly looks for the fulfilment of Old Testament prophecies in contemporary events in the Middle East (for further discussion of the problems associated with this approach, see 6.7.1 below). Both approaches recognize that the prophetic books are the inspired words of God with a significance that extends beyond their original context and that they are thus important for the people of God AD as well as BC; the issue, therefore, is not *whether* the prophecies apply to today but *how* (Goldingay, 2011: 305). The *Late Great Planet Earth* approach assumes that the prophets speak directly *of* our age, and thus looks for the fulfilment of their words in the events of our time. A paradigmatic approach, on the other hand, assumes that the prophets speak directly *to* our age (just as they speak to every age) but focuses on what the text reveals about who God is, how he relates to his people and what he expects of his people.

Practically, this means that we should consider the following kinds of questions when we seek to preach from the prophetic writings:

1 How is God's character and activity portrayed in this passage? Why does God intend to act in this fashion?
2 What is God calling people to be and do in this passage? Why are they called to act in this fashion?
3 What is paradigmatic in this passage?
4 In the light of the above, how might we expect God to be at work in our world today? How might this text shape the life and faith of the people of God today?

---

[10] H. Lindsay and C. Carlson, *The Late Great Planet Earth* (Grand Rapids: Zondervan, 1970).

6.5 Select the appropriate prophetic message[11]

As we have already seen in Chapter 2, the prophetic books are highly situational. They do not present general, systematic truths that could have been taught to any group in any place in any era but specific messages directed to concrete contexts. Amos addresses Israelites living in the northern kingdom in the eighth century BC, Jeremiah addresses the citizens of Judah living in and around Jerusalem in the seventh and sixth centuries BC, and Ezekiel the people of God in exile in Babylonia in the sixth century BC. Each of these prophets had a specific message for a specific people dealing with specific problems.

As a result we will find that the prophetic books sometimes speak with more than one voice on a given issue; when compared, the prophets may bring apparently opposing or competing messages, depending on the situation of their audience. For example, Isaiah can say to the people of Judah in the eighth century BC: 'Do not think that God has abandoned you. God will not let Jerusalem be captured. God is committed to Jerusalem', whereas just over a century later Jeremiah will announce, 'Do not think that God is committed to Jerusalem. God is going to let it be captured. God has abandoned you' (Goldingay, 1995: 190). The reason for these different messages is clear. Isaiah was addressing an audience which was terrified of the looming Assyrian menace and required divine encouragement. Jeremiah, on the other hand, was addressing an audience whose members had become so blind to their own sin they refused to believe God would come in judgement. Different situations, different messages.

The implication of this phenomenon for preaching from the prophets is that the preacher has to discern carefully the situation of his or her listeners and identify the appropriate message they need to hear on this basis. Contrasting situations should call forth different messages. If we preach Isaiah's message to the kind of congregation that Jeremiah addressed (or vice versa), we may end up perpetuating and reinforcing the problems which are already present instead of addressing and dealing with these appropriately. At times, we will need to build up and plant; at others we will need to uproot and tear down (Jer. 1.6).

> Scripture itself addresses a wide variety of contexts, and it is quite possible (for instance) to bring scriptural words of comfort to people whom scripture needs to disturb, or to make scriptural demands in situations where scripture would be more inclined to offer encouragement. That is to be a false prophet ... Merely to repeat things that the Bible itself says does not make us biblical preachers. The significance of biblical statements depends on the way they were designed to 'cut.' (Goldingay, 1995: 273)

The situational nature of the prophetic literature also means that, at a given point in time, some passages will speak more directly to our churches than

---

[11] My thinking for this section has been significantly shaped by Goldingay, 1995, esp. chs 12 and 17.

others. While we affirm that all of the prophetic literature is God's inspired word, this does not mean that we can equally apply every prophetic passage to every situation our churches may be facing. This is a reality that we see elsewhere in the Scriptures: the psalms of lament, for example, speak into different times and situations from the psalms of thanksgiving. Thus, we need to be careful of simply assuming that every prophetic passage will be directly relevant to the situation of our congregation just because it is part of the word of God.

> It is a consequence of scripture speaking directly to the situation of its day that it does not speak directly to ours. God paid this price in speaking specifically to the people living in their concrete situations. What God said directly to them may not be immediately intelligible [or applicable] to people living in other contexts. (Goldingay, 1995: 282)

At the same time, we need to be cautious and considered in making decisions regarding the relevance of passages, recognizing that such verdicts should not be set in stone. 'Passages cannot be identified once and for all as of specific or indirect relevance; they tend to change places as the circumstances of the church change' (Goldingay, 1995: 271).

For those who are engaged in regular preaching from the prophets, it is worth considering the balance between judgement and hope, critique and comfort in our sermons. While one of these emphases may be more pertinent at a given time, ultimately both elements should be present in our proclamation and ministry. Even Amos – perhaps the most pessimistic prophetic book in the entire Old Testament – finishes with a word of hope (9.11–15). It is easy for people who are constantly rebuked and berated to grow disillusioned and for despondency to set in. (Or for them simply to grow deaf to the cries of the prophets, a problem apparently also experienced by the ancient people of God; cf. Zech. 1.4.) An excessive emphasis on comfort and hope, on the other hand, may leave our people content in their situations, blind to their own sins and thus open to the negative consequences which may ensue (a problem also experienced by the ancient people of God; cf. Jer. 8.10–13). Both elements – rebuke and comfort – are found within the prophetic message, and problems can arise when one is practised at the expense of the other.[12]

6.6 Consider the witness of the New Testament

In this book, we have been concerned with hearing the prophets in their own context – in light of their own historical-cultural, theological and rhetorical worlds. This is appropriate and important. Given their location within the Old Testament canon, Christians affirm that the prophets are a significant element of the inspired word of God for the Church. Therefore,

---

[12] The twin elements I have identified (rebuke and comfort) connect well with Brueggemann's claim that Israel's prophets performed a twofold role: 'criticizing' and 'energizing'. For further discussion, see Brueggemann, 2001, esp. pp. 1–20.

we must be willing to listen carefully to this word as it was originally spoken, and not misconstrue its message by rushing ahead to link the Old Testament text simplistically with some New Testament text or to import a New Testament meaning into it.

> We must preach the Old Testament text itself for in its pages we are brought 'face to face with the Father of our Lord Jesus Christ and in the encounter God speaks . . . calling, exhorting, warning, judging, condemning, confronting and sanctifying.' In and of itself the Old Testament is a valuable witness to what it means to believe in this God.   (Gloer, 1987: 453, citing Terence Fretheim)

The Church, however, is not ancient Israel; we are not the prophet's original audience. We live on the other side of the cross, and this reality must shape the way we read and preach from these texts. Therefore, we should avoid jumping straight from the world of the prophets to the contemporary world, as tempting as it may be. Instead, the prophetic revelation must be taken through the lens of the New Testament to see what light it sheds on the themes, ideas and critiques the prophets raise. To put it bluntly, we cannot let the prophets themselves have the last word: to preach a sermon on an Old Testament prophetic passage without considering the teaching of the New Testament means that we are not engaging in truly *Christian* proclamation. We may discover that at times the New Testament does little to alter the essential prophetic proclamation (e.g. a passage condemning idolatry will find little opposition in the New Testament), and thus there may be no pressing need to refer explicitly to the New Testament within the sermon. On other occasions (e.g. when we are dealing with passages connected with the land or Temple), however, the movements and shifts of emphasis which we find within the New Testament are extremely significant and thus cannot be ignored. A valuable resource for working through this process is a topical or thematic biblical theology such as Scobie, 2003 or Alexander and Rosner, 2000.

Have you considered?
PAIRING OLD TESTAMENT AND NEW TESTAMENT TEXTS

Achtemeier (1989: 56–9) advocates a process of pairing (i.e. linking) Old Testament with New Testament texts as a means of providing a broader canonical perspective for hearing a single passage from the Old Testament. Five key criteria are frequently employed for identifying paired texts.* Texts can be paired on the basis of:

1 *A schema of promise and fulfilment.* The preacher looks for passages in the New Testament which explicitly or implicitly refer back to and fulfil the Old Testament prophecy (note, however, some of the problems identified with this approach outlined in 6.7.2 below).

2 *Analogy.* As discussed above, appropriate analogies are important for preaching the prophetic message. In this instance, however, the goal is not to identify analogies in the contemporary world, but analogous passages within the New Testament. For example, the preacher may identify a New Testament text which illumines or illustrates the way in which the Church's relation to God under the new covenant is similar to Israel's under the Sinai Covenant.

3 *Common motifs.* A motif is essentially a recurring textual element (e.g. a repeated word, phrase or concept). Examples include the references to 'living water' which we find in Jeremiah 2; 17 and John 4; 7, or '(good) shepherd' in Ezekiel 34 and John 10.

4 *Common thought.* Here, the two Testaments mutually illuminate each other.

5 *Contrast.* Old Testament and New Testament texts may be contrasted with each other – in some cases the New Testament may address the same topic or issue as the Old Testament passage but approach this from a different perspective or with a different emphasis (e.g. life after death). This can make for fertile preaching ground; however, 'this pairing device must be used cautiously, lest the Old Testament be presented as superseded by the New' (Achtemeier, 1989: 58).

---

* Lectionaries can help in the process of identifying paired texts.

6.7 Potential problems to avoid

So far in this chapter I have essentially advocated a paradigmatic approach to preaching from the prophets. This approach recognizes that the prophetic books (a) addressed an audience who lived at a different time and place from our own, and yet (b) contain a message which has the potential to address audiences living at different times and places, including our own. There are two other approaches that are commonly utilized for preaching from the prophets, which I will refer to as the contemporary fulfilment approach and the promise-fulfilment approach. Both of these approaches tend to ignore (at least) one of these elements, (a) and/or (b), and are thus potentially problematic if adopted as the sole or primary means for preaching from the prophets.

6.7.1 The contemporary fulfilment approach[13]

As we saw earlier, in 1970 Hal Lindsay (with C. Carlson) wrote a popular and widely influential book entitled *The Late Great Planet Earth*.[14] This book is based on a hermeneutical approach which assumes that the promises and

---

[13] For further critical engagement with this approach, see Goldingay, 2011: 297–310.

[14] *The Late Great Planet Earth* has sold more than 15 million copies according to the book's publisher (Zondervan). *The New York Times* recognized the book as the number one non-fiction best-seller of the 1970s (<http://zondervan.com/9780310277712>, accessed 18 October 2013). Some people, however, may question whether the categorization 'non-fiction' is, in fact, appropriate.

warnings which we find in the prophetic books must come true, i.e. they must be fulfilled in a literal sense, because we are dealing with the words of God. Advocates of this approach suggest that since we are living in the 'end times', we should expect those prophecies that have not yet literally come to pass (e.g. the glorious new Temple described in Ezekiel 40—48) to be fulfilled in our own day. Therefore, the goal of prophetic preaching is to identify such contemporary fulfilments and to warn people of their implications.

There are four key problems with this approach:

1 *It denies the incarnational nature of Scripture.* It thus fails to appreciate the characteristic way in which God reveals himself to his people – God has always revealed himself throughout history in ways which were comprehensible, accessible and relevant to his intended audience. In other words, God spoke through Moses in a way which second-millennium Hebrews travelling from Egypt to the promised land could understand. God spoke through Amos to get the attention of eighth-century residents of the northern kingdom of Israel. Jesus spoke in a manner that was (largely) comprehensible to his first-century Jewish audience.

   Therefore, I think it is appropriate to assume that the prophetic and apocalyptic authors also spoke in a way that was meaningful to and understood by their initial audience, something which is difficult to reconcile with the contemporary fulfilment approach. To say that God was not speaking about twenty-first-century events in these texts is *not* to deny that God could have done so, if he had wanted to. It is, rather, to assert that this would be uncharacteristic of the way in which the God of the Bible acts; this is not his standard *modus operandi*.

   The theological reason for denying the contemporary fulfilment approach is that

   > the God of the Bible characteristically speaks contextually, into situations rather than independently of them. He reveals key truths about the End that are relevant to people's present lives. He declines to give information about the future of a concrete or dated kind, insisting that people live by faith.
   >
   > (Goldingay, 1989: 321)

   It is difficult to see why the God of the Bible would reveal detailed events of the twenty-first century to people living in the first millennium BC (what relevance would it have to them?), even though he could have done so.

2 *It limits the relevance of the biblical text.* Ironically, in their attempts to emphasize the Bible's contemporary relevance, proponents of such an approach actually end up making the texts less relevant to the vast majority of the population (and, effectively, to all previous and ensuing generations). If we simply assume that the visions are coded previews of contemporary events in the Middle East, we can potentially deprive these texts of their power to speak a word of encouragement and hope to people enduring crises

or oppression, no matter when or where they live. For example, if we conclude that the 'king of the south' of Daniel 11.5 is only a reference to militant Islamic forces or the ruler of Egypt, we may fail to grasp how this material can function paradigmatically, shedding light on the nature of evil and opposition to God in general, and thus speaking into the lives and situations of people who are suffering persecution under all kinds of oppressive regimes, whether in China, Myanmar or Palestine. The contemporary fulfilment approach thus limits rather than liberates the text from speaking into a variety of contexts.[15]

3 *It fails to account sufficiently for the contingent nature of prophecy.* In Jeremiah 18 the Lord asserts that the prophetic word is not irrevocable or absolute but may be contingent on human response:

> At one moment I may declare concerning a nation or a kingdom, that I will pluck up and break down and destroy it, but if that nation, concerning which I have spoken, turns from its evil, I will change my mind about the disaster that I intended to bring on it. And at another moment I may declare concerning a nation or a kingdom that I will build and plant it, but if it does evil in my sight, not listening to my voice, then I will change my mind about the good that I had intended to do to it. (Jer. 18.7–10)

This is a dynamic which we see at play, for example, in the book of Jonah: after Jonah announces his message of imminent judgement (3.4), the citizens of Nineveh repent and thus the Lord decides not to enact the judgement he had announced (3.10). 'The warnings and promises are part of a living relationship between God and Israel; whether or not they are fulfilled depends on the reaction of those who receive them' (Goldingay, 1995: 192). This means that we cannot assume (contra *The Late Great Planet Earth* advocates) that *all* the prophetic words of the Old Testament *must* come to pass in the form in which they were given. A change on the part of Israel or the nations may have caused God to modify or even decide not to go through with the plan he had announced.

4 *It implies that all of the prophecies which have not yet been fulfilled apply at the same time (i.e. now or the near future).* Yet it is quite clear that Old Testament prophecy is, by its very nature, time bound. Throughout the Old Testament many different promises and warnings were given to Israel; they did not all apply at the same time (Goldingay, 2011: 307, 309). Some spoke to Israel while the people were in the land, others while they were in exile, still others when they had returned to the land but were a shadow of the nation they had once been. We cannot assume that prophecies which were originally uttered in another time and place apply today; the time when they were given and to which they historically relate is important.

---

[15] Furthermore, this approach implies that the prophetic books were not relevant for previous generations of Christians, as we are only seeing the fulfilment of their words in our day. If this approach is adopted, it is hard to see how the prophetic texts could have been 'useful for teaching, for reproof, for correction, and for training in righteousness' (2 Tim. 3.16) for our ancestors in the faith.

The *Late Great Planet Earth* approach, however, ignores this dynamic by 'flattening' all prophecies essentially into one time period (the now), and thus operates with a model or pattern of fulfilment which is not supported by the biblical text itself.

6.7.2 The promise-fulfilment approach

Another common hermeneutical approach within some elements of the Church, both contemporary and historic, is based on the assumption that the primary role of Israel's prophets was to predict the coming of Jesus the Christ. Such an approach draws its inspiration from the New Testament itself, whose authors regularly see Jesus as the fulfilment of Old Testament prophecy. The first two chapters of the Gospel of Matthew, in particular, repeatedly emphasize how Jesus' birth and early life could be understand in the light of Old Testament prophecies (note the presence of the 'fulfilment formula' in 1.22–23; 2.15, 17–18).

This hermeneutical approach finds expression in sermons whose primary intention is to explain how Jesus fulfils various Old Testament prophecies, with the preacher jumping immediately and directly from the text of the Old Testament (which may or may not be understood according to its historical and literary context) to the person and ministry of Jesus. When preachers use this approach they can sometimes leave the hearer with the impression 'that the Hebrew writers had preview videotapes of Jesus Christ playing on the screens of their minds as they penned their foretelling' (Allen and Holbert, 1995: 27).

These sermons often have one key goal: to show how God has been faithful to his promises. Listeners are thereby invited to strengthen their faith and trust in God – since God has proven himself to be reliable in the past, God can be trusted in the present, and there is a basis for hope in the future (Bos, 2008: 53).[16] Such sermons may also have an explicitly apologetic purpose, in which case the goal of the preacher is to use fulfilled prophecy as a means of establishing the veracity of the Scriptures and thus invite faith in the God who has authored them.

Such an approach is not necessarily problematic in and of itself. As it is popularly practised, however, this method carries with it a number of potential drawbacks.[17] For example, when we adopt a promise-fulfilment schema it is easy to lose sight of the meaning and significance of the words of the prophets for their own time. The tendency to jump straight from Old Testament 'predictions' to their New Testament fulfilment means that little consideration

---

[16] As Goldingay points out, however, faith that requires such 'props' (i.e. external verification) may not be true faith at all (1995: 161). It is certainly not the kind of faith for which the prophets call, i.e. a trusting hope and confidence that we are safe in God's hands, no matter how the circumstances or 'evidence' appear.

[17] Furthermore, the fact that the New Testament authors themselves read and utilized Old Testament prophetic texts in a number of different ways should caution us against adopting the promise-fulfilment schema as our default or only approach to preaching from the prophets. For further discussion, see Beale, 2012, esp. ch. 4.

is usually paid to the significance of the prophetic message for its original audience, the ancient Israelites.[18] We thus fail to hear the prophetic word as it was intended – as the word of God addressed to a specific situation in the life of God's people. 'This obviously enormous theological attempt to come to terms with the heritage of the Old Testament is in danger of losing it completely, because it can no longer present the message which it has to give' (Gunneweg, 1978: 26).

Pushed further, we could suggest that such a methodology effectively renders proclamation from the Old Testament irrelevant. Why would we want to preach from the Old Testament if the 'fuller music of God is heard in the New Testament' (Allen and Holbert, 1995: 16)? Thus, a strange irony results: this approach to preaching the prophets is often adopted out of a desire to show the relevance of the Old Testament text (it predicts Christ), yet it ultimately renders the text irrelevant (if we live on the other side of the prediction's fulfilment, what good is the prediction itself any more?).

Going deeper:
BAUMGÄRTEL ON THE EXISTENTIAL IRRELEVANCE OF TYPOLOGICAL AND PROMISE-FULFILMENT APPROACHES TO THE PREACHING OF OLD TESTAMENT PROPHECY

Friedrich Baumgärtel has raised a number of objections to the typological interpretation of the Old Testament which are also pertinent for the promise-fulfilment approach. In particular, he has highlighted its existential irrelevance – such an approach does not necessarily address the situation of the contemporary hearer. It is worth considering his argument in full even though we may disagree with elements of it:

> A demonstration that New Testament events are foreshadowed in the Old Testament does not affect my own existence, or rather, it forces me into the role of an intellectual onlooker. The insight that there is a correspondence between the New Testament event and its foreshadowing in the Old Testament does not matter and does not concern me in the slightest . . . I can only look at typological correspondences in a detached way; they are quite irrelevant to my life of faith. The type lacks the element of facticity, quite naturally, because facticity implies an action by God towards me and with me. The types are not events, but abstractions. In the types God acts neither towards Israel nor towards me. The types were inaccessible to Israel; they could only be seen in the light of Christ, and the Old Testament knows nothing of that. Nor do they have any compelling power for me as a Christian, because that is true only of God's action in Christ.
>
> (Baumgärtel, cited in Gunneweg, 1978: 211)

---

[18] Furthermore, it is not uncommon for people who adopt such an approach to misinterpret the Old Testament text in their desire to identify prophecies which supposedly anticipate Christ. For example, it is unlikely that Isaiah 60.6 ('A multitude of camels shall cover you, the young camels of Midian and Ephah; all those from Sheba shall come. They shall bring gold and frankincense, and shall proclaim the praise of the LORD') is a prediction of the coming of the wise men to Bethlehem (contra Chrysostom).

A second potential problem with this approach is that it leaves little room for the contemporary listener in the text due to its christological emphasis (the primary focus is the fulfilment of Old Testament prophecy in the life and ministry *of Jesus*) (Bos, 2008: 52). Sermons based on this approach jump back and forth between the times of the prophets and the life of Jesus, leaving the congregation as spectators on the sidelines of what God has done in history. Such sermons may potentially leave the audience with the question: 'So what? This may all be interesting, but how is it important for my life in the here and now?'

The promise-fulfilment approach implies that Christ is the 'Rome' on all the roads of God's history with Israel, the nations and Creation: all the prophecies point to, and culminate in, him. On one level this is true (cf. 2 Cor. 1.20). But this reality does not mean that Moses and the prophets are, so to speak, 'exhausted; they didn't finish their speaking in the Christ-proclamation' (Bos, 2008: 142). The roads don't *end* with him. The New Testament authors themselves recognize that the prophetic texts continue to offer words, metaphors, images and paradigms for the proclamation of God's acts in the post-Incarnation period.

Take, for example, the words of Isaiah 42.6; 49.6, which were originally addressed to the Servant of the Lord in the context of the Babylonian exile:

> I am the LORD, I have called you in righteousness,
>   I have taken you by the hand and kept you;
> I have given you as a covenant to the people,
>   a light to the nations ...

> It is too light a thing that you should be my servant
>   to raise up the tribes of Jacob
>   and to restore the survivors of Israel;
> I will give you as a light to the nations,
>   that my salvation may reach to the end of the earth.

Luke applies these words and images to Jesus on two occasions (Luke 2.32; Acts 26.23), but in Acts 13.47 they are also used to describe and explain the role of Paul and Barnabas: 'For so the Lord has commanded us, saying, "I have set you to be a light for the Gentiles, so that you may bring salvation to the ends of the earth"' (Bos, 2008: 148). This example shows how Old Testament prophecies may continue to speak beyond the Christ event; they have resonances for Christ's followers. The implications for those who seek to preach from the prophetic oracles today are clear. We must not become so fixated on the possible fulfilment of these words in the life and ministry of Christ that we fail to grasp their ongoing significance for the life of the people of God today.

So how might this all work out in practice? Let's take Isaiah 7.1–17 as our example. Christian preachers have traditionally focused on verse 14 ('Therefore the Lord himself will give you a sign: the virgin will conceive and give birth to a son, and will call him Immanuel', NIV) as a prophetic foretelling of Jesus'

Figure 6.1 *The Nativity with the Prophets Isaiah and Ezekiel* by Duccio (1308–11)

Image provided by Eugene A / Wikimedia Commons.

virgin birth (see Fig. 6.1). Matthew certainly sees this text as being fulfilled in Jesus' conception (Matt. 1.23) and thus the traditional approach is one way in which the Isaianic text could be approached. But is it the only way? What other homiletical possibilities are present?

One possibility would involve locating the passage more closely within its historical and canonical contexts. Historically, Isaiah 7 is set during a time of dire peril for pre-exilic Judah – the kingdom is being threatened by the combined forces of Syria and Israel to join their rebellion against Assyria (7.1–2). In this context, the Lord speaks to Ahaz and requests that he asks for a sign from the Lord (vv. 10–11). Although Ahaz refuses the divine invitation (v. 12), leading to apparent divine frustration (v. 13), nevertheless the Lord promises that he will give a sign: a young woman will give birth to a son and he will be named Immanuel, which means 'God is with us' (v. 14). The sign thus functions both as a reaffirmation of the Lord's promise to protect his people and as a call to faith, a call to Ahaz to trust in God and his promises despite the circumstances. Importantly, God's promise that he will be with his people appears in similar situations elsewhere in both the Old and New Testaments. For example, we find it in Genesis 28.15 in the context of Jacob's flight from his brother Esau and departure from the promised land. We find it in Exodus 3.12 in the midst of the Lord's call for Moses to go down and confront Pharaoh, king of Egypt. We also find it as a key element in Jesus' commission to the early Christians to go out into the world and make disciples of all nations (Matt. 28.20). We even find it in the situation of Joseph's crisis in Matthew 1.18–25. When we consider Isaiah 7 in its broader historical and canonical contexts, the text emerges both as a word of comfort to the Church (the Lord promises to be with his people), and a call to trust in the Lord and his promises, no matter what challenging circumstances or problems we may be facing.

6.8 Summary

When discussing preaching from the prophets, it is common to focus on the proclamation (i.e. *speaking*) of the word. I would argue, however, that authentic and faithful prophetic *speaking* must first be preceded by careful and attentive *listening*. This kind of listening involves a commitment to hearing the text in all its foreignness, abrasiveness and life-giving power. It involves a commitment to discerning carefully the situation of our audience so that we can proclaim the appropriate message. It involves a commitment to listening to the theological dynamics of the text so that we might discern how God is at work and what God might want of his people today. It is only when we have engaged in this kind of careful, disciplined listening that we should seek to engage in prophetic speaking.

Further reading

Achtemeier, E. *Preaching from the Old Testament*. Louisville: WJKP, 1989.

Allen, R. and J. Holbert, *Holy Root, Holy Branches: Christian Preaching from the Old Testament*. Nashville: Abingdon, 1995.

Brueggemann, W. *The Prophetic Imagination*, 2nd edn. Minneapolis: Fortress, 2001.

Duvall, J. S. and J. D. Hays, *Grasping God's Word: A Hands-On Approach to Reading, Interpreting, and Applying the Bible*, 3rd edn. Grand Rapids: Zondervan, 2012.

Goldingay, J. *Models for Interpretation of Scripture*. Grand Rapids: Eerdmans, 1995.

Goldingay, J. 'Can We Read Prophecy in Light of the Newspaper?' in *Key Questions about Biblical Interpretation: Old Testament Answers*. Grand Rapids: Baker, 2011, pp. 297–310.

Robinson, H. *Biblical Preaching: The Development and Delivery of Expository Sermons*, 2nd edn. Grand Rapids: Baker, 2001.

Select bibliography

Achtemeier, E. *Preaching from the Old Testament*. Louisville: WJKP, 1989.

Achtemeier, E. *Preaching from the Minor Prophets*. Grand Rapids: Eerdmans, 1998a.

Achtemeier, E. *Preaching Hard Texts of the Old Testament*. Peabody: Hendrickson, 1998b.

Ahlström, G. *Royal Administration and National Religion in Ancient Palestine*, SHANE 1. Leiden: Brill, 1982.

Alexander, T. and B. Rosner (eds). *New Dictionary of Biblical Theology*. Downers Grove: IVP, 2000.

Allen, R. and J. Holbert. *Holy Root, Holy Branches: Christian Preaching from the Old Testament*. Nashville: Abingdon, 1995.

Alter, R. *The Art of Biblical Poetry*. New York: Basic Books, 1987.

Arnold, B. and B. Beyer. *Readings from the Ancient Near East: Primary Sources for Old Testament Study*. Grand Rapids: Baker, 2002.

Beale, G. *Handbook on the New Testament Use of the Old Testament: Exegesis and Interpretation*. Grand Rapids: Baker, 2012.

Bellinger, W. 'Zion', in Sakenfeld, K. (gen. ed.), *The New Interpreter's Dictionary of the Bible*, vol. 5. Nashville: Abingdon, 2009, pp. 985–6.

Blenkinsopp, J. *Sage, Priest, Prophet: Religious and Intellectual Leadership in Ancient Israel*, LAI. Louisville: WJKP, 1995.

Blenkinsopp, J. *A History of Prophecy in Israel*, revised and enlarged. Louisville: WJKP, 1996.

Block, D. 'Preaching Ezekiel', in Kent, G., P. Kissling and L. Turner (eds), *'He Began with Moses . . .' Preaching the Old Testament Today*. Nottingham: IVP, 2010, pp. 157–78.

Boda, M. 'Zechariah, Book of', in Sakenfeld, K. (gen. ed.), *The New Interpreter's Dictionary of the Bible*, vol. 5. Nashville: Abingdon, 2009, pp. 967–71.

Bos, R. *We Have Heard That God Is with You: Preaching the Old Testament*. Grand Rapids: Eerdmans, 2008.

Brown, J. *Scripture as Communication: Introducing Biblical Hermeneutics*. Grand Rapids: Baker, 2007.

Broyles, C. 'Interpreting the Old Testament: Principles and Steps', in Broyles, C. (ed.), *Interpreting the Old Testament: A Guide for Exegesis*. Grand Rapids: Baker, 2001a, pp. 13–62.

Broyles, C. 'Traditions, Intertextuality and Canon', in Broyles, C. (ed.), *Interpreting the Old Testament: A Guide for Exegesis*. Grand Rapids: Baker, 2001b, pp. 157–75.

Brueggemann, W. *The Prophetic Imagination*, 2nd edn. Minneapolis: Fortress, 2001.

Brueggemann, W. 'Preaching as Reimagination', in Day, D., J. Astley and L. Francis (eds), *A Reader On Preaching: Making Connections*. Farnham: Ashgate, 2005, pp. 17–29.

Bullock, C. *An Introduction to the Old Testament Prophetic Books*, updated edition. Chicago: Moody, 2007.

Campbell, E. 'A Land Divided: Judah and Israel from the Death of Solomon to the Fall of Samaria', in Coogan, M. (ed.), *The Oxford History of the Biblical World*. Oxford: Oxford University Press, 1998, pp. 206–41.

Chalmers, A. *Exploring the Religion of Ancient Israel: Prophet, Priest, Sage and People*. London: SPCK and Downers Grove: IVP, 2012.

Charlesworth, J. (ed.). *The Old Testament Pseudepigrapha, vol. 1: Apocalyptic Literature and Testaments*. New York: Doubleday, 1983.

Cogan, M. 'Sennacherib's Siege of Jerusalem (2.119B)', in Hallo, W. (gen. ed.), *The Context of Scripture*, vol. 2. Leiden: Brill, 2003, pp. 302–3.

Collins, J. *Daniel*, Hermeneia. Minneapolis: Fortress, 1993.

Collins, J. (ed.). *Apocalypse: The Morphology of a Biblical Genre*, Semeia 14. Missoula: SBL, 1979.

Collins, T. *The Mantle of Elijah: The Redaction Criticism of the Prophetical Books*, BS 20. Sheffield: JSOT Press, 1993.

Coogan, M. *The Old Testament: A Historical and Literary Introduction to the Hebrew Scriptures*, 2nd edn. Oxford: Oxford University Press, 2010.

Cook, S. *Prophecy and Apocalypticism: The Postexilic Social Setting*. Minneapolis: Fortress, 1995.

Cook, S. *The Apocalyptic Literature*, IBT. Nashville: Abingdon, 2003.

Deppe, D. *All Roads Lead to the Text: Eight Methods of Inquiry into the Bible*. Grand Rapids: Eerdmans, 2011.

Duvall, J. S. and J. D. Hays. *Grasping God's Word: A Hands-On Approach to Reading, Interpreting, and Applying the Bible*, 3rd edn. Grand Rapids: Zondervan, 2012.

Farris, S. 'Bridging Then and Now,' in Wilson, P. (gen. ed.), *The New Interpreter's Handbook of Preaching*. Nashville: Abingdon, 2008, pp. 179–81.

Fee, G. and D. Stuart, *How to Read the Bible for All Its Worth*, 3rd edn. Grand Rapids: Zondervan, 2003.

Gloer, W. 'Preaching from Malachi', *Review and Expositor* 84/3 (1987): 453–64.

Golden, M. *Migrations of the Heart*. New York: Anchor Press, 1983.

Goldingay, J. *Daniel*, WBC. Dallas: Word Books, 1989.

Goldingay, J. *Models for Interpretation of Scripture*. Grand Rapids: Eerdmans, 1995.

Goldingay, J. *Key Questions about Biblical Interpretation: Old Testament Answers*. Grand Rapids: Baker, 2011.

Gordon, R. *The Place Is Too Small for Us: The Israelite Prophets in Recent Scholarship*, SBTS 5. Winona Lake: Eisenbrauns, 1995.

Gorman, M. *Elements of Biblical Exegesis: A Basic Guide for Students and Ministers*. Peabody: Hendrickson, 2001.

Gowan, D. *Theology of the Prophetic Books: The Death and Resurrection of Israel*. Louisville: WJKP, 1998.

Grabbe, L. *Priests, Prophets, Diviners, Sages: A Socio-Historical Study of Religious Specialists in Ancient Israel*. Valley Forge: Trinity Press, 1995.

Gravett, S., K. Bohmbach, F. Greifenhagen and D. Polaski. *An Introduction to the Hebrew Bible: A Thematic Approach*. Louisville: WJKP, 2008.

Gunneweg, A. *Understanding the Old Testament*, OTL. London: SCM Press, 1978.

Hallo, W. (gen. ed.). *The Context of Scripture*, vols 1–3. Leiden: Brill, 2003.

Hanson, P. *Old Testament Apocalyptic*, IBT. Nashville: Abingdon, 1987.

Hays, J. D. *The Message of the Prophets: A Survey of the Prophetic and Apocalyptic Books of the Old Testament*. Grand Rapids: Zondervan, 2010.

Healey, J. 'Mot', in van der Toorn, K., B. Becking and P. van der Horst (eds), *Dictionary of Deities and Demons in the Bible*, 2nd edn. Leiden: Brill, 1999, pp. 598–603.

Hewitt, C. 'Guidelines to the Interpretation of Daniel and Revelation', in Amerding, C. and W. Gasque (eds), *A Guide to Biblical Prophecy*. Peabody: Hendrickson, 1977, pp. 101–16.

Huffmon, H. 'Prophecy (ANE)', in Freedman, D. N. (ed.), *Anchor Bible Dictionary*, vol. 5. New York: Doubleday, 1992, pp. 477–82.

Huffmon, H. 'The Expansion of Prophecy in the Mari Archives: New Texts, New Readings, New Information', in Gitay, Y. (ed.), *Prophecy and Prophets: The Diversity of Contemporary Issues in Scholarship*, SBL Semeia Studies. Atlanta: Scholars Press, 1997, pp. 7–23.

Hutton, R. *Charisma and Authority in Israelite Society*. Minneapolis: Fortress, 1994.

King, P. 'Jerusalem', in Freedman, D. N. (ed.), *Anchor Bible Dictionary*, vol. 3. New York: Doubleday, 1992, pp. 747–66.

Klein, W., C. Blomberg and R. Hubbard, *Introduction to Biblical Interpretation*, rev. edn. Nashville: Thomas Nelson, 2004.

Lang, B. *Monotheism and the Prophetic Minority: An Essay in Biblical History and Sociology*, SWBAS 1. Sheffield: Almond Press, 1983.

Leclerc, T. *Introduction to the Prophets: Their Stories, Sayings and Scrolls*. New York: Paulist, 2007.

Leith, M. 'Israel among the Nations: The Persian Period', in Coogan, M. (ed.), *The Oxford History of the Biblical World*. Oxford: Oxford University Press, 1998, pp. 276–316.

LeMon, J. and B. Strawn, 'Parallelism', in Longman III, T. and P. Enns (eds), *Dictionary of the Old Testament: Wisdom, Poetry and Writings*. Downers Grove: IVP, 2008, pp. 502–15.

Levenson, J. *Sinai and Zion: An Entry into the Jewish Bible*. New York: HarperCollins, 1987.

Levenson, J. 'Zion Traditions', in Freedman, D. N. (ed.), *Anchor Bible Dictionary*, vol. 6. New York: Doubleday, 1992, pp. 1098–102.

Lindblom, J. *Prophecy in Ancient Israel*. Oxford: Basil Blackwell, 1963.

Lindsay, H. *There's a New World Coming: An In-Depth Analysis of the Book of Revelation*. Eugene: Harvest, 1984.

Lindsay, H. and C. Carlson, *The Late Great Planet Earth*. Grand Rapids: Zondervan, 1970.

Lipiński, E. 'סגלה *s^egullā*', in Botterweck, G., H. Ringgren and H-J. Fabry (eds), *Theological Dictionary of the Old Testament*, vol. 10, trans. D. Stott. Grand Rapids: Eerdmans, 1999, pp. 144–8.

Lipiński, E. 'צפון *ṣāpôn*', in Botterweck, G., H. Ringgren and H-J. Fabry (eds), *Theological Dictionary of the Old Testament*, vol. 12, trans. D. Stott. Grand Rapids: Eerdmans, 2003, pp. 435–43.

Lundbom, J. *The Hebrew Prophets: An Introduction*. Minneapolis: Fortress, 2010.

Matthews, V. *The Hebrew Prophets and Their Social World: An Introduction*, 2nd edn. Grand Rapids: Baker, 2012.

Matthews, V. and D. Benjamin, *Social World of Ancient Israel, 1250–587 BC*. Peabody: Hendrickson, 1993.

Mays, J. *Amos*, OTL. London: SCM Press, 1969.

McConville, G. *Exploring the Old Testament, vol. 4: Prophets*. London: SPCK, 2002.

McKenzie, S. *Covenant*, UBT. St Louis: Chalice, 2000.

Meier, S. *Themes and Transformations in Old Testament Prophecy*. Downers Grove: IVP, 2009.

Mendenhall, G. and G. Herion, 'Covenant', in Freedman, D. N. (ed.), *Anchor Bible Dictionary*, vol. 1. New York: Doubleday, 1992, pp. 1179–202.

Millard, A. 'Writing and Prophecy', in Boda, M. and J. G. McConville (eds), *Dictionary of the Old Testament: Prophets*. Downers Grove: IVP, 2012, pp. 883–8.

Miller, P. *The Religion of Ancient Israel*, LAI. Louisville: WJKP, 2000.

Mobley, G. *The Return of the Chaos Monster: And Other Backstories of the Bible*. Grand Rapids: Eerdmans, 2012.

Moore, M. and B. Kelle. *Biblical History and Israel's Past: The Changing Study of the Bible and History*. Grand Rapids: Eerdmans, 2011.

Mowvley, H. *Guide to Old Testament Prophecy*. Guildford: Lutterworth, 1979.

Müller, H. 'נביא *nābî''*, in Botterweck, G., H. Ringgren and H-J. Fabry (eds), *Theological Dictionary of the Old Testament*, vol. 9, trans. D. Green. Grand Rapids: Eerdmans, 1998, pp. 129–50.

Murphy, F. *Apocalypticism in the Bible and Its World: A Comprehensive Introduction*. Grand Rapids: Baker, 2012.

Nissinen, M. *Prophets and Prophecy in the Ancient Near East*, SBLWAW 12. Atlanta: SBL, 2003.

Osborne, G. *The Hermeneutical Spiral*, 2nd edn. Downers Grove: IVP, 2006.

Otto, E. 'ציון *ṣîyôn'*, in Botterweck, G., H. Ringgren and H-J. Fabry (eds), *Theological Dictionary of the Old Testament*, vol. 12, trans. D. Stott. Grand Rapids: Eerdmans, 2003, pp. 333–65.

Petersen, D. 'Rethinking the Nature of Prophetic Literature', in Gitay, Y. (ed.), *Prophecy and Prophets: The Diversity of Contemporary Issues in Scholarship*, SBL Semeia Studies. Atlanta: Scholars Press, 1997, pp. 23–40.

Petersen, D. 'Prophet, Prophecy', in Sakenfeld, K. (gen. ed.), *The New Interpreter's Dictionary of the Bible*, vol. 4. Nashville: Abingdon, 2009, pp. 622–48.

Preuss, H. D. *Old Testament Theology*, vol. 1. Edinburgh: T&T Clark, 1995.

Preuss, H. D. *Old Testament Theology*, vol. 2. Edinburgh: T&T Clark, 1996.

Pritchard, J. (ed.), *Ancient Near Eastern Texts Relating to the Old Testament*, 3rd edn with supp. Princeton: Princeton University Press, 1969.

Provan, I., V. P. Long and T. Longman III, *A Biblical History of Israel*. Louisville: WJKP, 2003.

von Rad, G. *Old Testament Theology, vol. 2: The Theology of Israel's Prophetic Traditions*. Edinburgh and London: Oliver and Boyd, 1965.

Rast, W. *Tradition History and the Old Testament*, GBSOTS. Philadelphia: Fortress, 1972.

Rata, T. 'Covenant', in Boda, M. and J. G. McConville (eds), *Dictionary of the Old Testament: Prophets*. Downers Grove: IVP, 2012, pp. 99–105.

Redditt, P. *Introduction to the Prophets*. Grand Rapids: Eerdmans, 2008.

Redditt, P. 'Editorial/Redaction Criticism', in Boda, M. and J. G. McConville (eds), *Dictionary of the Old Testament: Prophets*. Downers Grove: IVP, 2012, pp. 171–8.

'rhetoric'. *Collins English Dictionary – Complete and Unabridged 10th Edition*. HarperCollins (<http://dictionary.reference.com/browse/rhetoric>, accessed 15 December 2013).

Ricoeur, P. 'The Metaphorical Process as Cognition, Imagination, and Feeling', *Critical Inquiry* 5/1 (1978): 143–59.

Roberts, J. 'Zion Tradition', in Sakenfeld, K. (gen. ed.), *The New Interpreter's Dictionary of the Bible*, vol. 5. Nashville: Abingdon, 2009, pp. 987–8.

Robertson, O. P. *The Christ of the Prophets*. Phillipsburg: P&R Publishing, 2004.

Rofé, A. *Introduction to the Prophetic Literature*, BS 21. Sheffield: Sheffield Academic Press, 1997.

Russell, D. S. *Prophecy and the Apocalyptic Dream: Protest and Promise*. Peabody: Hendrickson, 1994.

Ryken, L. *Words of Delight: A Literary Introduction to the Bible*, 2nd edn. Grand Rapids: Baker, 1992.

Ryken, L., J. Wilhoit and T. Longman III (gen. eds), *Dictionary of Biblical Imagery*. Downers Grove: IVP, 1998.

Sandy, D. B. *Plowshares and Pruning Hooks: Rethinking the Language of Biblical Prophecy and Apocalyptic*. Downers Grove: IVP, 2002.

Sandy, D. B. and R. Giese (eds). *Cracking Old Testament Codes: A Guide to Interpreting the Literary Genres of the Old Testament*. Nashville: Broadman and Holman, 1995.

Sawyer, R. *Prophecy and the Biblical Prophets*, rev. edn. Oxford: Oxford University Press, 1993.

Scobie, C. *The Ways of Our God: An Approach to Biblical Theology*. Grand Rapids: Eerdmans, 2003.

Smith, M. *The Early History of God: Yahweh and the Other Deities in Ancient Israel*, 2nd edn, BRS. Grand Rapids: Eerdmans, 2002.

Steck, O. *Old Testament Exegesis: A Guide to the Methodology*, SBLRBS 33. Atlanta: Scholars Press, 1995.

Stökl, J. 'Ancient Near Eastern Prophecy', in Boda, M. and J. G. McConville (eds), *Dictionary of the Old Testament: Prophets*. Downers Grove: IVP, 2012a, pp. 16–24.

Stökl, J. *Prophecy in the Ancient Near East: A Philological and Sociological Comparison*, CHANE 56. Leiden: Brill, 2012b.

Stromberg, J. 'Formation of the Prophetic Books', in Boda, M. and J. G. McConville (eds), *Dictionary of the Old Testament: Prophets*. Downers Grove: IVP, 2012, pp. 271–9.

Strong, J. 'Zion: Theology of', in VanGemeren, W. (ed.), *New International Dictionary of Old Testament Theology and Exegesis*, vol. 4. Grand Rapids: Zondervan, 1997, pp. 1314–21.

Stuart, D. *Old Testament Exegesis: A Handbook for Students and Pastors*, 4th edn. Louisville: WJKP, 2009.

Sweeney, M. *The Prophetic Literature*, IBT. Nashville: Abingdon, 2005.

Tate, W. *Biblical Interpretation: An Integrated Approach*, 3rd edn. Grand Rapids: Baker, 2008.

Thompson, D. 'Oracles for Our Community: Preaching from the Old Testament Prophets', *Preaching Today* (<http://www.preachingtoday.com/skills/themes/propheticpreaching/oraclesourcommunity.html>, accessed 4 October 2013).

van der Toorn, K. 'From the Mouth of the Prophet: The Literary Fixation of Jeremiah's Prophecies in the Context of the Ancient Near East', in Kaltner, J. and L. Stulman (eds), *Inspired Speech: Prophecy in the Ancient Near East, Essays in Honor of Herbert B. Huffmon*. London: Continuum, 2004.

Towner, W. 'The Preacher in the Lions' Den', in Mays, J. and P. Achtemeier (eds), *Interpreting the Prophets*. Philadelphia: Fortress, 1987, pp. 273–84.

Troxel, R. *Prophetic Literature: From Oracles to Books*. Chichester: Wiley-Blackwell, 2012.

Tucker, G. *Form Criticism of the Old Testament*, GBSOTS. Philadelphia: Fortress, 1971.

Waltke, B. with C. Yu, *An Old Testament Theology: An Exegetical, Canonical, and Thematic Approach*. Grand Rapids: Zondervan, 2007.

Walton, J. *Ancient Near Eastern Thought and the Old Testament: Introducing the Conceptual World of the Hebrew Bible*. Grand Rapids: Baker, 2006.

Ward, J. and C. Ward, *Preaching from the Prophets*. Nashville: Abingdon, 2005.

Watson, W. *Classical Hebrew Poetry: A Guide to Its Techniques*, T&T Clark Biblical Languages. London: T&T Clark, 2005.

Williams, M. 'Contemporizing', in Wilson, P. (gen. ed.), *The New Interpreter's Handbook of Preaching*. Nashville: Abingdon, 2008, pp. 182–5.

Williamson, P. *Sealed with an Oath: Covenant in God's Unfolding Purpose*, NSBT 23. Downers Grove: IVP, 2007.

Wilson, R. *Prophecy and Society in Ancient Israel*. Philadelphia: Fortress, 1980.

Wilson, R. 'Notes on 1 and 2 Kings', in Meeks, W. (ed.), *The HarperCollins Study Bible*. New York: HarperCollins, 1993, pp. 509–604.

Wolff, H. 'Prophecy from the Eighth through the Fifth Century', in Mays, J. and P. Achtemeier (eds), *Interpreting the Prophets*. Philadelphia: Fortress, 1987, pp. 14–26.

Wood, L. *The Prophets of Israel*. Grand Rapids: Baker, 1998.

Wyatt, N. *Religious Texts from Ugarit: The Words of Ilimilku and His Colleagues*, BS 53. Sheffield: Sheffield Academic Press, 1998.

Scripture index

Subject index

Did you know that SPCK is a registered charity?

As well as publishing great books by leading Christian authors, we also . . .

. . . make assemblies meaningful and fun for over a million children by running www.assemblies.org.uk, a popular website that provides free assembly scripts for teachers. For many children, school assembly is the only contact they have with Christian faith and culture, and the only time in their week for spiritual reflection.

. . . help prisoners become confident readers with our easy-to-read stories. Poor literacy is a huge barrier to rehabilitation. Prisoners identify with the believable heroes of our gritty fiction, but questions at the end of each chapter help them to examine their choices from a moral perspective and to build their reading confidence.

. . . support student ministers overseas in their training. We give them free, specially written theology books, the International Study Guides. These books really do make a difference, not just to students but to ministers and, through them, to a whole community.

Please support these great schemes: visit www.spck.org.uk/support-us to find out more.